THE PORTION OF THE POOR

THE PORTION OF THE POOR

Good News to the Poor
in the Wesleyan Tradition

Edited by
M. Douglas Meeks

KINGSWOOD BOOKS

An Imprint of Abingdon Press
Nashville, Tennessee

Library of Congress Cataloging-in-Publication Data

The portion of the poor: good news to the poor in the Wesleyan tradition / edited by M. Douglas Meeks.
    p.   cm.
    Papers presented at the Oxford Institute of Methodist Theological Studies at Sommerville College, Oxford, England, in the summer of 1992–Galley p. 7.
    Includes bibliographical references.
    ISBN 0-687-15529-0 (alk. paper)
    1.Church work with the poor–Methodist Church–Congresses. 2. Methodist Church–Doctrines–Congresses. I. Meeks, M. Douglas. II. Oxford Institute of Methodist Theological Studies (9th: 1992: Sommerville College)
BX8347.P67   1994
261.8'325'08827–dc20
                                          94-36367
                                             CIP

Unless otherwise noted, all Scripture quotations are from the New Revised Standard Version Bible, copyright © 1989 by the Division of Christian Education of the National Council of the Churches of Christ in the USA. Used by permission.

The Scripture quotations noted RSV are from the Revised Standard Version of the Bible, copyright © 1946, 1952, 1971 by the Division of Christian Education of the National Council of the Churches of Christ in the USA. Used by permission.

The diagram on p. 73 is reproduced from Donald F. Durnbaugh, *The Believers' Church: The History and Character of Radical Protestantism* (Scottdale, PA: Herald Press, 1985), p. 31. Used by permission.

Portions of Chapter Eight were first published in the "Introduction" to *A Song for the Poor: Hymns by Charles Wesley*, ed. S T Kimbrough, Jr. (New York: Mission Education and Cultivation Program Department of the General Board of Global Ministries, The United Methodist Church, 1993), pp. 1–16. Used by permission.

This book is printed on acid-free recycled paper.

95 96 97 98 99 00 01 02 03 04 — 10 9 8 7 6 5 4 3 2 1

Manufactured in the United States of America

Dedicated to

Donald H. Treese

In gratitude for his outstanding service to the
Oxford Institute of Methodist Theological Studies

Contents

On Reading Wesley with the Poor

M. Douglas Meeks

The essays comprising this book were originally given as papers at the Oxford Institute of Methodist Theological Studies at Sommerville College, Oxford, England in the summer of 1992. The theme of the Institute was "Good News to the Poor in the Wesleyan Tradition." The premise of the Institute was threefold: (1) that in some sense God's relation to the poor is constitutive of the gospel as conveyed by John Wesley and the Wesleyan tradition; (2) that honestly facing the deformation of the Wesleyan tradition away from the poor would be a hard but necessary task requisite to its more faithful practice; and (3) that regaining an evangelical relationship to the poor would be decisive for the transformation and renewal of Methodist/Wesleyan churches across the world. As can be readily seen, the essays presented here do not flinch in pursuing all aspects of the premise with verve. These fresh readings of the Wesleyan tradition from the perspective of the poor result in penetrating questions and incisive suggestions as to work that must be done in service of the generations of the people called Methodists.

Wesley and the Poor

While there is some controversy as to whether "the poor" meant for Wesley those poor among his own movement or the poor at large in society, none of the essayists doubts Wesley's unequivocal insistence that the poor are at the heart of the evangel and that life with the poor is constitutive of Christian discipleship. There is widespread agreement that, according to the practice of Wesley, "the poor in Jesus Christ" has to do with the nature of the church and with salvation. Wesley's ministry with the poor included feeding, clothing, housing the poor; preparing the unemployed for work and finding them employment; visiting the poor sick and prisoners; devising new forms of health care education and delivery for the indigent; distributing books to the needy; and raising structural questions about an economy that produced poverty.

Wesley's turn to the poor, however, was not simply *service of* the poor, but more importantly *life with* the poor. Whether Wesley would have "naturally" preferred to be among the prosperous or the poor can be debated, but that he actually shared the life of the poor in significant ways, even to the point of contracting diseases from their beds, is undeniable. Nor was Wesley's life with the poor merely an accident of his peculiar gifts. Rather Wesley understood visiting the poor as an essential means of grace necessary to the continuance of faith. To be in Christ meant to take the form of Christ's own life for and with the poor. To be a disciple of Christ meant to be obedient to Christ's command to feed his sheep and to serve the least of his sisters and brothers. This meant that the *evangel* took Wesley where the poor were, in the fields and hamlets, mines and city streets, where enclosures and a mercantilist economy had made them congregate.

The Poor in an Economy of Death

If to be a Methodist in Wesley's view is to practice life with the poor as the heart of Christian discipline, what does it mean to look into the face of today's poor? Victorio Araya-Guillén writes from the perspective of Latin America's observance of the 500th anniversary of the European conquest of Latin America and its consequences in the holocaust of millions of indigenous peoples, the enslavement of African peoples brought to the "new world," and the destruction of the environment. Araya-Guillén confronts the Wesleyan churches with the threatened holocaust of the poor in our time: "How are we to be a community of faith in a world of injustice and death for the poor? How do we announce, by deed or word, the good news of life that comes from God (John 10:10) in the midst of this bad news of the daily death of the poor who are victims of the economic rationale imposed by the West?"

Poverty is not the will of God or the incorrigible result of fate. Mortal poverty is not due to the sins of the poor. Poverty as we know it today, this "new sacrifice to the Moloch of greed," as Araya-Guillén says, is an historic, social, and economic act that has a beginning and

10

objective causes with economic mechanisms and social subjects. It responds objectively to a process that is determined by "reason" and the will of human beings. It is a complex process that was developed from the Renaissance mercantile expansion (during the sixteenth century) to today's international neoliberal capitalism (the new free market economy). Within this process, thanks to unequal exchange, some countries "specialize in gaining and others in losing" until today there are clearly "the losers," throw-away nations.

In the new situation of market capitalism spreading throughout the world the poor are increasingly subjected to the laws and necessities of the market and free trade. In the economic "logic" of capitalism, capital and the laws of the market come first. Human beings and the satisfaction of their basic needs and the right to life for all come second. This is true also in First World countries as capital flight causes a restructuring that means many are dropping out of the middle-class while the plight of the poor becomes more desperate.

No one may assume that Wesley or the Wesleyan tradition can solve the economic quandaries that entail the terribly complicated conditions of poverty's death-dealing in our time. And yet if the Wesleyan legacy has nothing to contribute to the life and future of the poor, it forfeits its right to re-present Jesus Christ in the *oikoumene*.

Contradictions in the Wesleyan Legacy

How then can the Methodist memory be brought to bear on the life and death situation of the poor today? Wesley seems to have made life with the poor a dimension of discipleship without which one's salvation is endangered. But has the Wesleyan heritage been so compromised that it is useless today in confronting the threatened holocaust of the poor?

Itemelung Mosala writes out of the South African situation in which the leading forces on almost all sides do not allow the poor to speak for themselves. Methodism, he argues, is of necessity a people's movement which at its best has nurtured poor people's spirituality for liberation. But the way the Wesleyan tradition has actually played itself out has been a "part of the history of domination and exploitation" of the poor. His question is whether the Wesleyan tradition can be retrieved and practiced in such a way that it can actually represent the voice and action of the poor. The answer is not so facilely given.

One unmistakable learning of the Ninth Oxford Institute is that there are profound ambiguities, contradictions, and instabilities in the Wesleyan tradition regarding the gospel and the poor. In an highly nuanced essay, Donald Dayton searches for a new historiography by which the fundamental intention buried in the history of Methodism can be critically retrieved. Dayton believes that Wesley held together elements that have been fragmented over the last two centuries into various branches of Methodism. Once the "subtle synthesis" is fractured, the resulting Methodist strands convey "only certain fragments of the tradition that disenfranchise and excommunicate each other as reflections of themes that cannot be genuinely 'Wesleyan.'" Profound sociological and psychological forces of *embourgeoisement* have pulled various branches of Methodism away from the poor and toward the "respectable" center of the culture.

Our best chance for finding the integrity of Wesley's own emphasis on "good news to the poor," according to Dayton, is to regard the "underside" of Methodist history in those branches that have not succumbed to the dominant culture and political economy. Thus Dayton surveys such traditions as the African Methodist Episcopal Church, Primitive Methodism, Free Methodists in North America, and even the Salvation Army and Latin American Pentecostalism. These traditions generally express a gospel egalitarianism, full ministry of women and lay, and a lifestyle that enabled evangelization to the masses. For Dayton there is a clear "correlation between the countervailing movement toward the poor and away from them with the theological fragmentation of Methodism." One way to begin dealing with this theological fragmentation is learning to reread the Bible.

Toward a Wesleyan Biblical Hermeneutic

There are many problems in developing a Wesleyan hermeneutic of the scriptures today. For one thing Wesley was not liberated from the practices of pre-modernity. As he works at a hermeneutic from the perspective of the black South African poor, Mosala suggests that a much more serious problem is reading the poor within the biblical texts. His question is "how to interpret the eloquence with which the poor are silent and the absence through which they are present in the pages of the Bible." Focusing on the Exodus story of Moses and the midwives, he asks whether the text itself is open to the misuse to which colonizers and oppressors have put the exodus narrative. He argues that the most difficult aspect of Exodus is the absence of the slaves's own voices. A non-oppressed person, Moses, becomes the hero of the oppressed. If, as some scholars claim, this Exodus material was compiled during the Solomonic reign, then is the story not simply an ideology condoning the dispossession of peasants and slave labor practiced by the regime of Solomon?

Such a story can be liberated only through the praxis of the poor against their present enslavement; and only in this way can the stories themselves be liberating. It is the everyday praxis of the poor who gain their spirituality from the Bible which Mosala would like to retrieve from the best of the Wesleyan tradition: "For without this new presence of the poor in the business of reading the Bible, there is no recovering the erstwhile presence of the poor in the stories of the Bible."

Overcoming Wesleyan Theological Fragmentation

In view of the massive dimensions of world poverty today, the internal ambiguities of the Methodist tradition, and the difficulties of reading the poor in the Bible and the Bible with the poor, how can we critically practice the Wesleyan tradition today?

These essays raise penetrating questions about the theology that must be done afresh today in service of a critical practice of the Wesleyan tradition. Did Wesley adequately establish "good news to the poor" in the being of God so that the evangelical emphasis on the poor has sufficient theological grounding? Two authors, Theodore Jennings and Donald Dayton, argue that while Wesley intended such a theological claim, he did not consistently succeed. The failure to provide this theological grounding in a normative way, it is argued, led to the pervasive "constitutional instability" concerning the poor in the Methodist tradition. And thus the case is made for the urgency of christological, pneumatological, and trinitarian work that must be done today, work that will more clearly demonstrate the biblical grounding of the gospel to the poor in the life and being of the Triune God.

The essays of David Lowes Watson and Richard P. Heitzenrater make significant contributions to this task on the christological level. Watson criticizes the prevailing mode of evangelism for its failure to proclaim the fullness of Christ's work in all his offices. The priestly

13

and prophetic offices tend to get divided up by conservative and liberal evangelistic approaches to the near exclusion of the sovereign office. Watson argues that to hold together the Wesleyan proclamation of the gospel to the poor requires holding together all aspects of the work of Christ. To emphasize only the forgiveness and reconciliation of the priestly office is to fall into the well-known antinomianism which simply reinforces the individualism of persons and the isolation of communities. To emphasize only the prophetic office leads to an activism that is soon devoured by despair. According to Watson, the true power by which we can live good news to the poor comes from the power of God's own love of God's children. This is not a love without judgment but is "above all the royal summons to prepare for audience with a wrathful parental potentate whose children have been neglected and starved and beaten and slaughtered for millennia. On that day of God's anger, we shall all tremble for a long, long time."

Heitzenrater asks the questions, Why was Wesley so interested in helping and going among the poor? What was Wesley's motivation for working with the poor? The answers, Heitzenrater believes, can be found in a christologically-grounded virtue ethics. Wesley held a virtue ethic that emphasized *being* in Jesus Christ rather than *doing* as response to a command. Sanctification was basically a form of meditative piety through which the virtues in Jesus Christ were implanted in the disciple. To imitate Jesus Christ meant not only to see Jesus as the model of life but also in him to find the power to live with the poor. Heitzenrater makes clear the connection between life in Christ and acts of love toward the poor. "The simple answer, then, to the question, Why did Wesley work with the poor? is, first and foremost, because Jesus did so, but also because Jesus told him to do so and would help him to do so."

Personal Piety and Social Transformation

Several of the essays, especially those of Rebecca Chopp and Theodore Jennings, concentrate on the relationship between personal and social transformation in the Wesleyan emphasis on *scriptural holiness*. The grammar of sanctification is not simply reconciliation, but "emancipatory transformation." While criticizing the privatistic and moralistic tendencies of the Wesleyan tradition,

Chopp and Jennings reformulate both the discourses of grace and sin in historical and structural terms.

In the dialectic between denouncing sin and announcing grace the work of the Holy Spirit is interdependently personal and social. According to Jennings, "it was precisely Wesley's pietism, his own evangelical fervor, his own moralizing scrupulosity that gave his social ethic an immediate plausibility." If persons are to make a genuine difference in the conditions of an economy that oppresses the poor, they must be freed from their own idolatrous captivities and practice the disciplines of "evangelical economics" in their own lives. Without the development of a personal and communal ethic of frugality, simplicity, generosity, and solidity with the poor no persons or communities will have the courage to challenge the "economy of death."

The Discourse of Sin

A Wesleyan theology that genuinely speaks of God's presence with the poor as grounded in God's own character and that demonstrates the personal and social dimensions of overcoming poverty will have to develop what Chopp calls a "very large doctrine of sin." Chopp calls on pragmatic future-oriented thinking and rhetoric tied to praxis to develop such a doctrine of sin.

The first task in such a doctrine of sin is simply to name suffering and lament it. The impoverishment of the church often has to do with its inability to see and be persuaded by the brokenness, deprivation, and death of human beings and of creation. Without lament, without suffering from suffering, there can be no doctrine of sin or of grace.

The next task of a doctrine of sin is to unmask and criticize the idolatries that get expressed in the ideologies and unjust systems of a society, that is to show the relationship between systems of injustice and the depth structure of sin. Such an analysis of the depth structure of idolatry is itself a resistance to sin and evil. As Chopp argues, "sin as idolatry is structural in the sense that it is embedded in the political practices, the everyday habits, the linguistic structures, the ways we are raised as whites, or blacks, or women or men." Such hidden structures determine the way politics and language exclude the poor from what they need to survive and flourish in the expression of their humanity.

15

A doctrine of sin should relate such structures to the depth of human depravity and original sin—otherwise Christian approaches to the poor become mere wishful thinking. But it is a distinctive mark of a Wesleyan doctrine of sin that whatever is known and said about sin is based on grace. This is particularly important in resisting the widespread tendency in market society to employ sin as an alibi for the continuance of sin. Thus it is argued that because the human being is inevitably greedy, we should accept the fated consequence of that greed in economics. Such a fatalism, of course, serves the interests of those who most benefit from existing arrangements and seems theologically to justify the subjection of the poor to death. A doctrine of sin, then, should lead to a focus on God's work in overcoming sin and to the possibilities of human life as defined by grace against sin. How are we not only justified but also sanctified by grace? How through the power of the Holy Spirit can we construct sanctified ways of living in the face of God and the poor? God's grace does not save us without changing us.

The Poor and the Future of the Methodist Project

The title of this volume is taken from a hymn of Charles Wesley. S T Kimbrough, Jr., reminds us that the worship and spiritual life of the Wesleyan movement gave expression to the life and saving work of God with the poor. Does the tradition of Wesleyan piety and theology suggest some different modalities in which the church might genuinely manifest good news to the poor? The deconstruction of traditions conveying ideologies that oppress the poor and the criticism of the idolatries expressed in the hegemonic culture can lead to nihilism if they are not accompanied by the constructive work of sanctification. What does God really hope for the poor? What do the poor hope for? In the lament of suffering from poverty is already the seed of hope for a life sufficient to express one's humanity on behalf of life.

Several of the essays presented here converge on the claim that the future of Methodism lies in recovering a concrete practice of "scriptural holiness." Scriptural holiness, set in the presence of the poor, means transformed habits, relationships, and ways of being in the world. Holy living in the presence of the poor means that our practices of property, work, and consumption would be radically changed. It means new ways of praying with the poor and reading

16

scripture with the poor. It also means practicing *diakonia* with the poor so that they are not made objects of ministry and thus robbed of their ministry.

The sanctifying grace of God in Jesus Christ is meant not just for the sinner but also for a society beset by structural sin. An ancient and persisting problem, of course, is that sanctifying grace can be mediated to the larger structures of society only through the life and work of communities. And yet the spread of the market society makes community ever more threatened. What in the Wesleyan tradition can contribute to the imagining and constructing of new forms of community? Can there be communities which are not defined by the ancient principle of "birds of a feather flock together?" Can sanctifying grace create community in which the boundaries move according to the presence of Jesus Christ in the stranger, the radically other? Could such a community actually be an adumbration of the reign of God in which the poor actually and concretely hear good news? The following essays invite the Wesleyan communion to answer these questions in the presence of the poor and of a groaning creation and under the power of God's grace that creates the joy of a home for the homeless.

Chapter 1

Wesley and the Poor: An Agenda for Wesleyans

Theodore W. Jennings, Jr.

Introduction

The main burden of this essay takes for granted the case I have made in my book *Good News to the Poor: John Wesley's Evangelical Economics*. On that basis I will argue for an agenda for Methodist theologians and scholars that may make effective for World Methodism a recuperation of this essentially Wesleyan theme: *Wesley's option for the poor*.

Wesley and the Poor

In order that we may become more clear about our Wesleyan heritage in this respect let us first recount Wesley's own appraisal of the character of the Methodist movement that he launched and directed for so many years.[1] Toward the end of his life Wesley attempted a number of assessments of his movement. In the sermon "The Signs of the Times," Wesley sought to place Methodism within his own growing appreciation of history as the arena of God's saving work. In order to show that God was indeed at work in history he pointed to the Methodist movement and declared: "And surely never in any age or nation, since the Apostles, have those words been so eminently fulfilled, 'the poor have the gospel preached unto them,' as it is at this day."[2]

Here we should notice two related things. The first is that the mission of the people called Methodists can be accurately summarized, according to Wesley, as the preaching of good news to the poor. The second is that this is regarded by Wesley as the fulfillment of the gospel mandate itself and thus as making of the people called Methodists a true sign of the purpose and work of God in the world.

Now we cannot understand the significance of Wesley's remark here unless we bear in mind that this carrying of good news to the poor was not, for Wesley, something that just happened. It was the result of a conscious and deliberate choice; Wesley turned away from the prosperous in order to turn toward the poor. Thus Wesley can say to his critics in the established church: "The honourable, the great, we are thoroughly willing to leave to you. Only let us alone with the poor, the vulgar, the base, the outcasts of men."[3] And Wesley is as good as his word. He regularly reports in his *Journal* that he was alarmed by the presence of the prosperous among his audience. When he discovered them there he would change his message to suit the occasion: "In the evening I was surprised to see, instead of some poor plain people, a room full of men daubed with gold and silver. That I might not go out of their depth, I began expounding the story of Dives and Lazarus."[4] And when a sermon on the rich man in hell appealing in vain for the mercy of the poor in God's reign does not suffice to drive the prosperous away, Wesley himself is disposed to leave: "Many of the rich and honourable were there; so that I found that it was time for me to fly away. . . ."[5] It would be possible to illustrate this point many times from Wesley's *Journal*. He seeks out the poor, he turns away from the prosperous. There are still many who regard such a policy as perverse, but Wesley understood that it was absolutely necessary if the gospel of Christ were to be served. When he was questioned about this policy Wesley responded: "Religion must not go from the greatest to the least, or the power would appear to be of men."[6]

Here is what we may call the theological basis of Wesley's preferential option for the poor in the work of evangelization. Religion, if it is not to be the pious form of worldliness, if it is instead to be the response to the action of God, must begin where God begins, among the poor, the despised, the oppressed, and the marginalized. Otherwise it is not a divine but a merely human project, in which case, whatever success such worldly evangelism has need not be explained as the operation of God but as the result of good public relations, market research, and customer satisfaction. Wesley understood that the means must correspond with the end, that evangelization which corresponds to the gospel must begin with the poor. Wesley was far from ignorant of the plight of the poor; indeed he made it a regular practice to acquaint himself directly with their situation. He was not content to preach to them, even though his favorite venues for preaching (open fields, market places, public hangings, etc.) made certain that he would reach them in ways closed to those who stayed within the bounds of churches and meeting halls. Instead Wesley made a point of visiting the poor and even of lodging with them, as we are so vividly reminded in the work of John Walsh.[7]

The practice of visiting the poor on a regular and constant basis goes back to Wesley's Oxford days. He regarded it then simply as an essential aspect of that holiness without which none can see God. He could no more imagine a week without visiting the hovels of the poor than he could a week without participation in the Eucharist. Moreover, he insisted to all who placed themselves under his direction that the visiting of the poor was an essential means of grace and an indispensable form of obedience to the command of Christ: "The walking herein is essentially necessary, as to the continuance of that faith whereby we are saved by grace, so to the attainment of everlasting salvation."[8]

Wesley understood that the deep class divisions of his own society were largely based upon a studied ignorance of the life of the poor on the part of the prosperous. "One great reason why the rich in general have so little sympathy for the poor is because they so seldom visit them."[9] Thus the practice of the visitation of the poor which he regarded as essential to Methodist discipline was a practice that broke down the barriers between the classes so as to produce a conversion of the prosperous to the cause of the poor. An immediate consequence of this intimate awareness of the conditions of poverty was the determination to develop programs of aid for the poor: "On the following days, I visited many of our poor, to see with my own eyes what their wants were, and how they might be effectually relieved."[10] One level of response was the practice of "begging for the poor." Here is one illustration of this practice which comes from Wesley's 82nd (!) year:

> At this season [Christmas] we usually distribute coals and bread among the poor of the society [of London]. But I now considered, they wanted clothes as well as food. So on this and the four following days, I walked through the town, and begged two hundred pounds in order to clothe them that needed it most. But it was hard work, as most of the streets were filled with melting snow,

which often lay ankle deep; so that my feet were steeped in snow-water nearly from morning till evening.[11]

Wesley also made a point of the fact that the collections taken at his public meetings were not for Church buildings nor for pastors' salaries but for the poor. Even at this level, Wesley's practice far exceeded what is normally thought of as alms giving and charity.

But he went much further than this; he sought to help the poor help themselves. Thus he organized clinics, cooperatives, and credit unions. He understood the evangelization of the poor to entail far more than simply preaching to people. The gospel concerns not a disembodied word but the word made flesh. And the announcement of good news to the poor must at the same time be the enactment of good news to the poor, the healing of broken bodies, and the feeding of the hungry, and the mobilizing of the paralyzed. If this does not occur there can be no talk of an evangelism that has anything to do with the gospel of Jesus Christ.

Wesley sought to make the welfare of the poor the criterion of every aspect of the Methodist movement. This is already obvious in his choice of venue for preaching. It is also the motivation for his work of extensive publishing of small tracts and abridgements and indeed whole libraries. It is the criterion for the building of meeting places which were to be cheap so as not to make the Methodists beholden to the rich:

> Let all preaching-houses be built plain and decent; but not more expensive than is absolutely unavoidable: Otherwise the necessity of raising money will make rich men necessary to us. But if so, we must be dependent upon them, yea and governed by them. And then farewell all Methodist discipline, if not doctrine too.[12]

Thus every aspect of Methodism was subjected to the criterion, How will this benefit the poor? Solidarity with the poor was not to be a side issue, but the test of every dimension of activity.

One other aspect of Wesley's preaching and practice that is critical to the evangelization of the poor is the style of life that corresponds to a commitment to the poor. From the days at Oxford, Wesley had sought to develop a lifestyle that would permit him to engage in solidarity with the poor. This included not only visitation but also the disciplines of frugality. When Methodism became a lay ecumenical movement following 1738, Wesley developed his views on this question under such headings as stewardship and in specialized reflections on such matters as dress, the drinking of tea, and so on. Wesley maintains that we are to be stewards "of God and the poor."[13] Stewardship for the poor means that everything beyond what is necessary for life belongs to the poor. God gives me what I have in order that I may give it to the poor. Wesley writes:

> . . . who lodged [this money] for a time in your hands as his stewards; informing you at the same time for what purposes he entrusted you with it? Do not you know that God entrusted you with that money (all above what buys necessaries for your family) to feed the hungry, to clothe the naked, to help the stranger, the widow, the fatherless; and indeed, as far as it will go, to relieve the wants of all mankind.[14]

Given that our economic life is to governed by the welfare of the poor, the attempt to acquire more than is necessary, and especially the consumption of surplus, is to be understood as robbery. Thus consumption or needless expense is simply the robbery of the poor. Wesley's view of what we would call consumerism is as strict as a commandment: "Everything about thee which cost more than Christian duty required thee to lay out is the blood of the poor."[15]

When Wesley speaks of stewardship, he is not talking about fund raising for a middle-class institution. He is talking about the redistribution of wealth from the prosperous to the poor. Now much of this concerns what we would call personal ethics, but Wesley's own reflections on these matters do not stay at the level of the personal and individual. His concern for the poor leads him into direct conflict with powerful sectors of his own society: the medical and legal professions. It leads him to denounce ordinary business practices as sheer robbery. His identification with the poor and despised of society makes it possible for him to read history and society from the underside. It is this which enables him to see the ghastly character of the slave trade and vigorously to oppose the policies of colonialism.

I am aware that Wesley's views on what I have called his evangelical economics have certain limitations from the point of view of our own more sophisticated understanding of global economic reality. It is the case that Wesley was a man of the eighteenth century rather than our own. I do not suppose that it is possible to transplant the early modern reflections of Wesley into the post modern context in which we must live, reflect, and work. As José Míguez Bonino and others have reminded us, not only have the concrete realities of our world altered and the sociological, psychological, and philosophical categories within which that reality is reflected and criticized, but even the theological categories and hermeneutical principles that guide our work have also dramatically changed.[16]

Yet still, I believe Wesley may speak challengingly to us in our own time. When, after years of avoiding the study of Wesley, I found it necessary to teach Wesley in Spanish to seminary students in Mexico, I discovered that they found in Wesley a point of entry to the concerns of liberation theology which a traditional reading of scripture and a pious suspicion of Marxist theory had conspired to close off to them. That is, Wesley's concrete concern for the poor, his critique of wealth and privilege, his protest against colonialism and exploitation made a far greater impact upon them than the more sophisticated and undoubtedly more conceptually adequate formulations of contemporary Latin American theologians. I think it was precisely Wesley's own pietism, his own evangelical fervor, and his own moralizing scrupulosity that gave his social ethic an immediate plausibility that provoked a rethinking of the gospel and a re-reading of their own situation. I have found this experience repeated in a variety of other contexts as well. Indeed, I regularly find that Wesley, despite his limitations, is still quite radical for those who are committed either to a nineteenth-century tradition of piety or to the institutional maintenance of an established church.

The resistance on the part of the institutional church to Wesley's commitment to the poor and the apoplexy engendered by a discounting of the priority of Aldersgate are negative indications of the power of a rereading of Wesley just as the conscientization and mobilization of the poor and of those who work with the poor facilitated by this re-reading suggests to me that this project is not simply a waste of time. Who can doubt that this challenge is an urgent one today? For it is becoming increasingly clear that the anti-evangelical economics of institutionalized greed and violence is destroying the earth and its inhabitants. During the Nazi horror twelve million victims, half of them Jews, were sacrificed to national pride and institutionalized insanity. But in the decade of the 1980s one hundred million children died of poverty. One hundred million! Each year more children die of poverty (of starvation, malnutrition, and the diseases that feed on the starving) than the Nazi horror machine could exterminate in all the years of its feverish and fiendish activity. Each year there is a new holocaust, a new sacrifice to the

24

Moloch of greed and indifference. This slaughter of the innocents is no fortuitous calamity but the direct result of economic arrangements which blind us to reality by making us complicitous in calamity.

Mortal poverty is not due, as some blasphemously maintain, to an act of God. It is the work of our economic idolatry.[17] The earth, reeling as it is, produces more than enough food to feed plentifully every man, woman, and child on the planet. Yet our economic system produces murderous scarcity. A few have more than they can consume, so much that garbage disposal is a critical problem, while millions perish in sight of plenty. One nation, containing a tiny fraction of the earth's population (the majority of whom think of themselves as Christians), consumes half the earth's resources yet still manages not to feed its own hungry. If proposals are made to remedy this iniquitous hoarding and waste by the few at the expense of the many we are told that this would destroy the economy. The economy of death. That is an economy worthy of destruction; it is open contempt of God.

This same economy of death imposes upon poor nations the crushing burden of debt, extorting interest payments by which poorer nations subsidize the excesses of richer nations. Thus the countries of Latin America, for example, so far from receiving aid from their immensely wealthy neighbor, actually export capital. Meanwhile the banks and international lending agencies propose that in order to solve the "debt crisis" the poorer countries accept "loans," the effect of which is to increase their debt and their payments of interest to these same banks. The International Monetary Fund has the audacity to extract as the price of this "aid" that the poor countries actually reduce their assistance to the poor of their own nation, cutting back food assistance to the hungry, medical care to the dying, education for the illiterate in order to have the honor of continuing to subsidize the wealthiest nation on earth. Neither Latin bureaucrats nor international bankers, nor the technocrats who negotiate these "final solutions" pay a penny. On the contrary, they grow wealthy creating and solving the "debt" crisis. It is only the poor who pay.

The solvency of the international financial market is the blood of the poor. The peoples of eastern Europe, so recently delivered from political tyranny, find themselves now remorselessly delivered up into the hands of this same economy of death that has been leeching the life blood of Africa, Latin America, and Oceania. The same economy of death diverts human resources and those of the planet to the creation of weapons of death to ensure the security of the greedy and the complacent. Vast sums are squandered on unproductive arms industries even by the poorest nations, or rather by the elites of those nations, in imitation of their wealthier cousins of the North. Thus the instability generated by the greed of the few and the impoverishment of the many induces the greedy to protect themselves from the many, thereby reducing the resources available to redress the grievances of the many, thereby further destabilizing the societies they pretend to protect.

The vicious cycle of impoverishment and violence feeds upon itself. This same economy of death meanwhile is rapidly destroying the earth itself. More than half the arable land of the globe has already been turned into desert by the agriculture of avarice, arrogance, and ignorance. The waters of the earth are becoming cesspools, the air poisonous. Where once forests stood to cleanse the air and make it healthful for all creatures, there is now drifting sand; where grassy plains stretched to the horizons to feed the creatures of the earth there is now only desert. The prophets promise that the deserts can be made to bloom like gardens, but the economy of death turns the garden that remains into a desert. Already the majority of the earth's plant and animal species have been exterminated.

Is there no remedy? Certainly no minor adjustments to this mechanism of death will transform it into something that nourishes life. Without a radical transformation of our ways of dealing with one another and the earth, God's teeming creation may become a lifeless rock hurtling through the void of space. But from whence can such a radical transformation come?

A Future for a Wesleyan Perspective

In my judgment the outline of an answer is to be discerned in the gospel of Jesus Christ. Those of us in the Wesleyan traditions may be helped to discern aspects of this gospel through a reflection on Wesley. Recently our world has been shaken by the great earthquake to the East and the collapse of the Soviet empire. Indeed some believe that a similar seismic event is in store for the post-Maoist regime that still governs more than a quarter of the earth's population. What is to be made of all this? Are we to imagine as Francis Fukyama has maintained, that we live at the end of history? Does the collapse of

Communism in the East portend the hegemony of capitalism with or without a trickle down effect? What shape the New World Order? Are we condemned to the economic reign of avarice limited only by a formal democracy vitiated by the marketing of political double talk? These are not only rhetorical questions.

For about a century the opposition to the dominion of avarice has been largely carried by Marxism. Marxism has been the carrier first of a radical critique of those arrangements that make the world safe for the oligarchs and a buffering middle class at the expense of the impoverished masses of human kind. The Marxist critique has served as a powerful instrument in the demystification of the ideological disguises by which the interest of the powerful has wrapped itself in the stolen robes of the common good. Moreover, Marxism has also been the bearer of the aspiration of those classes which have been exploited, impoverished, and chained by the rule of unbridled mammon. Marx himself concentrated on the proletariat and Mao considered the peasant class. To be sure neither gave much attention to the truly destitute, the fully marginalized. And each perspective gave way to the domination of elites scarcely less malignant than their capitalist counterparts. Even though Marxism as a legitimating system for state and empire has been discredited, the historical project of which it has been the bearer is scarcely less urgent: that of unmasking the arrangements of greed and of carrying the hopes of the marginalized.

Indeed this is a project as old as the liberation of Egyptian slaves and the denunciations of the prophets. Historically this project has been carried by Israel, Christianity, Islam, and Marxism. Each in its own way has betrayed this project by becoming a legitimating system for the arrogation of power and privilege by the few at the expense of the many. In my view this is the true dynamic of history, a dynamic whose end is not the hegemony of avarice but the dominion of justice and generosity heralded by the prophets and made flesh in the mission and ministry of Jesus of Nazareth. In the current situation there is a renewed opportunity for the reassertion of an evangelical economics that measures political and economic systems by the criterion of the welfare of the discarded masses of humanity.

I do not suppose that we will find all the resources necessary for the continuation of this project under the conditions of post-modernity in the early modern reflections of Wesley. But there are several points of departure that I believe may be of use to us. When Wesley

27

provided an analysis of economic conditions in England he took as his point of departure the situation of the poor.[18] The specific economic policies, including trade and tax measures, that he proposed all had in view a response to the misery of the poor. Certainly any economic proposals that have a Wesleyan character today must likewise begin with the situation of the destitute and the dying. It is this rather than notions of development or free trade or gross national product that must be the beginning and end of economic policy if the economy of death is to be countered and overcome. Further we may recall that when Wesley came to oppose the slave trade and to assign responsibility for the moral outrage which that system perpetrated his analysis followed the money trail by asking: Who benefits, that is, Who is responsible?

Similarly, in an analysis of the economy of death today, it is important also to ask, Who benefits from the arrangements that consign the bulk of the earth's population to misery and dehumanization and death? When Wesley thought about social sin he thought about the globe and not simply the nation, thus his denunciation of the policies of colonialism not only by the Spanish in Latin America but also by the British in India. He knew the motive was profit and the price was the blood of the poor. One of the ways in which Christian social ethics in the first world is short-circuited is through a focus on a national situation in which those who suffer most are a minority of the population. We seldom see how our prosperity is purchased at the price of the misery of millions in places many of us cannot find on a map. The days of national economy have long passed away. We cannot afford to be more provincial than Wesley in seeing the connection between our prosperity and others' misery.

One of the things for which Wesley is often criticized is his failure to endorse the American revolution. Yet here, too, I think we may have a point of departure for fruitful reflection on the new world order. For Wesley saw that democracy in the case of the colonies was a mask for the interest of merchant princes and slave owners. He was not taken in by talk of human rights that only served the interests of the wealthy few, or talk of democracy that excluded the poor and women. We have forgotten the way in which democracy can all too readily be manipulated by the powerful for their own ends. It is important therefore as we reflect on the new world in which we live that we not be uncritical of the ways in which formal democracy serves as a cover for the perpetuation of the privilege of unscrupulous elites who have become adept at the manipulation of public opinion in a society of addictive consumption.

Finally I think we would do well not to dismiss Wesley's undoubted emphasis on the transformation of the person as an essential dimension of social transformation. Persons become willing tools of the economy of death when they have not been enabled to practice the disciplines of an evangelical economics in their own lives. The point of an emphasis on the personal is not to distract from the social but rather to capacitate persons for transformation at all levels of life. Only as we are freed from the ethos of consumption and as the barriers between prosperous and poor are broken down will we find both the courage and the capacity to challenge the economy of death. Thus I believe that the development of a personal and communal ethic of frugality and simplicity of life and of generosity to and solidarity with the poor is indispensable if we are to break the hold of the economy of death upon the hearts of the prosperous and the bodies of the destitute. For this revolution in consciousness and practice, the reflections of Wesley provide an indispensable resource.[19]

The transformation of our world entails, I think, a theory of transformation, a theology of transformation. Hence I want to turn our attention to the theological work that is necessary if we are to realize anew the promise of a Wesleyan reformation of church and society.

If theology is to respond to the Wesleyan and evangelical criterion of good news to the poor then it will be necessary to address certain themes adumbrated by Wesley but often obscured in subsequent theology. All too often the gospel we proclaim and upon which we reflect is one that interprets the world but does not alter it. This is especially true when we speak of grace and particularly, justifying grace. For here we too often speak of a grace that saves us without changing us. The emphasis on grace alone or faith alone then serves perfectly well as a palliative to the consciences of the prosperous. For God in this view really does not require justice but rather calls us just, treats us as if we were just, on condition merely that we in some way pay God the tribute of a willing suspension of disbelief, which we are pleased to call faith.

One of the most important contributions of Wesley is to utterly reject this interpretation of grace and faith. Wesley will have nothing to do with the sort of grace that saves us without changing us. Hence

Wesley's criticism of so-called Gospel Preachers: "But of all preaching, what is usually called Gospel preaching is the most useless, if not the most mischievous: a dull, yea, or lively, harangue on the sufferings of Christ, or salvation by faith, without strongly inculcating holiness. I see, more and more, that this naturally tends to drive holiness out of the world."[20] Whenever we speak of a genuine transformation we are likely to be warned not to minimize the seriousness of sin. The pervasiveness and profundity of sin in the human heart and condition is invoked to tell us why it is that all our talk of the transformation of life and society is simply wishful thinking, is uninformed concerning the depth of human depravity and original sin.

In spite of Wesley's "optimism of grace" he was by no means ignorant of the power of sin in human life. Indeed Wesley's longest theological treatise was precisely a defense of the doctrine of original sin. But here Wesley was on far sounder ground than many theologians of today. For he knew that the doctrine of original sin and even of total depravity cannot be deployed as an alibi for continuance in sin. The function of these doctrines is to show the necessity of grace, not to show the impotence of grace. One of the important fruits of late twentieth century theological labor is that we are learning to differentiate the kinds of sin from which human beings need deliverance. For many in the middle classes sin is a bondage to addictive behavior and compulsive denial of the truth about ourselves and our world. Theologies of liberation in Africa and Latin America have recovered a biblical view of the sin of oppression and injustice among the ruling classes. Korean Minjung theology opens a way for understanding how the sins of injustice poison the hearts of the oppressed with the bitterness, suppressed rage, and self-contempt that is called "han."[21]

The discrimination of the ways in which sin dominates our lives serves also to make clear the dimensions of liberation from sin's dominion that is promised us in Christ Jesus. An important aspect of a theology responsive to the cry of the impoverished and oppressed is to recover a clear view of the power of grace through faith to change lives, societies, and the world itself. This will mean unmasking incompetent theological tributes to the power of sin that mask a fatalism with respect to the world which only serves the interests of the current rulers of the world. One of the ways in which theology has often stopped itself short from becoming a liberating word is through puzzlement about the relationship of faith and works. This has especially characterized Protestant theology. Wesley had the good sense to be clear that faith and works are intimately related, indeed that faith is instrumental to the accomplishment of the divine will for a life of love:

> I would just add, that I regard even faith itself, not as an end, but as a means only. The end of the commandment is love, of every command, of the whole Christian dispensation. Let this love be attained, by whatever means, and I am content; I desire no more. All is well, if we love the Lord our God with all our heart and our neighbor as ourselves.[22]

Faith separated or even opposed to works serves the interest of the maintenance of the world as it is.

What Wesley lacked was a way of developing the relationship between faith and works in a truly satisfactory way. The result has been a certain instability in Wesleyan theology which hobbles between a Protestant proclamation of faith without works on the one hand and a fall into the petty works righteousness of degenerate holiness traditions on the other. What is needed in a Wesleyan theology is an understanding of faith that produces a real correspondence to the divine will without becoming trivial. I believe that this can be best achieved if we return to faith the connotation of faithfulness or fidelity.[23] Understood in this way faith in Christ will be expressed as faithfulness to his mission and ministry, loyalty to him and to the project of announcing and actualizing the reign of God as the reign of justice and generosity and joy. In this way we may succeed in making clear how it is that the sheer unmerited favor of God in Christ that befriends the outcasts of religious, economic, and political society awakens the astonished and glad response of joy and gratitude among these so as to engender a glad and joyful loyalty to the love that has befriended us. It is this loyalty of joyful and responsive love that seeks to imitate the love of the loving God and so becomes an imitation of the divine love made manifest in Christ.

On this basis it is possible to make clear how it is that faithfulness is by no means to be confused with the grim attempt to curry the favor of a tyrannical judge, or with the attempt to make something of oneself. In this sense the faithfulness that proceeds from the divine initiative has nothing to do with the old works righteousness even though it far more clearly does produce and necessarily produces

31

that holiness without which none shall see God. To be sure this entails a fundamental re-reading of Romans from the standpoint not of the perpetuation of the system of sin but from the perspective of those who yearn for the transformation.

The aim or goal of justification is the production of justice: just persons, just societies, a just earth. We must liberate theology from the Alice in Wonderland logic by which justification does not produce justice. Wesley, whatever the limits of his hermeneutics or his theological categories, would not accept this trifling with God that spoke of justification while leaving us in our sins, any more than it would make sense to speak of a resurrection of the dead that left us in our graves. While a reformulation of themes like sin and grace, justification and faith is crucial to meeting the challenge of a turn to the poor and dispossessed, it seems to me that the heart of Wesleyan theology is the notion of scriptural holiness. It is this which seems to provide the *cantus firmus* of Wesley's theology from the days in Oxford to the theological maturity of his later years. For it is the realization of holiness which is the project for which faith itself can be regarded as a means. We are all aware that there are dangers here. There is the danger of a holiness that collapses into petty moralizing, of an individualizing and legalizing of the Christian life that is surely unacceptable.

Wesley, despite his best efforts, did not always escape these difficulties. Yet in spite of his limitations Wesley did know that the aim of the divine grace was the restoration of the image of God whereby we become faithful images and reflections of the divine nature. He knew that the rules of the societies were to be regarded as only prudential helps along the way to the realization of this goal. Moreover, he was aware that holiness was not something that pertained to the individual in isolation but rather to the person in relationship and in community, and he was aware that the actualization of this holiness had in view the transformation of society as a whole. Further he knew that the key to the actualization of this holiness was an imitation of the divine orientation to the poor and the excluded. All of these things Wesley at his best knew. Yet he often lacked the hermeneutical tools or the theological categories to prevent the collapse of these insights into the moralistic legalisms that came to be the hallmark of Wesleyan and holiness movements generally. It is this degradation of the notion of holiness that has made it seem an unlikely candidate for serious theological reflection.

It is an urgent task for a Wesleyan theology to re-construct the idea of holiness as the practice of persons empowered by God to be imitators of God and so to be participants in the divine mission. This entails an imitation of the one who though he was rich, for our sakes became poor. It is then an embodiment of the practice of love that lives in sacrificial solidarity and unconditional generosity among those who are excluded by the religious and secular systems of deceit, destruction, and death. Holiness that is genuinely scriptural and even evangelical has nothing to do with the childish game of inventing arcane moralistic rules but is instead the imitation of the divine love under the concrete forms of social, political, economic and religious history. One cannot become more like God by withdrawing oneself from the world that God created, from the poor and despised whom God in Christ befriended, from the concrete forms of suffering and the dominion of death exposed by Christ's cross and invaded by his resurrection.

A further area of theological work in the Wesleyan spirit that may enable us to respond more adequately to the global economy of death has to do with reflection on the sphere of nature as the site of divine care and activity. It is in Wesley's late sermons on creation and new creation that his long-standing interest in the natural world is integrated into his theological reflection. Here it becomes clear that the aim of salvation entails a future not only for a few pious souls, but for forests and rivers, for mountains and meadows, for lions and tigers and house pets as well.[24] Indeed when a friend requested a kind of funeral service for his canine companion of many years, I was able to read for him at the gravesite the wonderful passage from "The General Deliverance."[25] This strong insistence upon the world of nature as the sphere not only of divine providential care but also as the sphere of redemption goes back to Wesley's beloved "Fathers" of the Church who insisted on the resurrection of the earth as ingredient to the consummation of the divine salvific aim.

This extension of the horizon of redemption (already anticipated, for example, in Romans) is an important counter to the tendency to regard nature as a mere stage for human achievement or as a treasure house of resources for our exploitation. Writing on the eve of the industrial revolution, Wesley did not perceive the full implication of this view of creation as the sphere of redemption, nor its connection to his evangelical economics including the option for the poor. But today we live in a world in which the connection between the impoverishment of the masses of humanity and the violation of the earth has become all too clear. The scars of sin's cruel reign are manifest in the bodies of the poor and the devastation of the earth and air and water. A Wesleyan theology will see in the earth not only the violated body of sin but also the scene of redemption. A Wesleyan theology of transformation which takes seriously the importance of future redemption becoming evident in present deliverance from the yoke of sin and death will issue not only in protest against the violation of the earth but also in the practice of transformation of the earth as evidence of the truth of the gospel.

I have suggested that the driving dynamic of history is the call for justice for the wretched of the earth. I believe that the people called Methodists may make a contribution to this historical project through a recuperation of Wesleyan themes of commitment to the poor and to the grace that transforms life and society. But it is not only theological and ethical work that is called for here but also historical work.

Obviously it is important for us as for all Christians to generate our theological and ethical proposals out of a conversation with the Bible. This after all was also Wesley's own principle. We are all well aware that Wesley's hermeneutics are not yet fully liberated from the habits of pre-modernity. He is an inveterate proof-texter, and even after he is forced to consider the whole of scripture in the preparation of his *Explanatory Notes* on the Old and the New Testament, he does not have available to him the tools for accomplishing what he clearly wished to accomplish: to see any point from the standpoint of the whole.

In my judgment the development of a new hermeneutics within the ambit of liberation theology makes possible a re-reading of the biblical texts that will strengthen a commitment to an evangelical economics. But contemporary hermeneutics not only provides us with a far greater range of data in the re-reading of the Bible from the standpoint of the poor; it also enables us to apply a kind of hermeneutics of suspicion to the reading of the biblical texts. For we are becoming aware of the ways in which the biblical texts already betray the effects of a de-radicalizing tendency, of an attempt to come to terms with the world rather than confront the world with the un-watered-down claims of the God of Exodus and of the Crucified.[26]

This willingness to criticize particular passages of scripture on the basis of the fundamental meaning of the gospel is not alien to the

Wesley who could dismiss the exegetical arguments for double pre-destination by asserting that it would be better to forget the Bible than believe that God was a monster. Wesley himself sought to re-read the Bible whole from the standpoint of his own mission and ministry among the poor and outcast of England. Today persons on several continents and with different constituencies among the marginalized of the earth are attempting the same. A Wesleyan re-reading of scripture today will join hands with these projects around the globe. In this re-reading of scripture we may be assisted, as Wesley was, by acquaintance with the exegesis of the earlier church theologians. Indeed many of the most radical passages that I quote from Wesley in *Good News to the Poor: John Wesley's Evangelical Economics* are echoes of passages from theologians like Basil and the Gregories and Chrysostrom. The splendid work by Justo González, *Faith and Wealth*, provides ready access to the teaching of the early church on what I have called evangelical economics.[27] A comparison of these texts with those that I have cited from Wesley will show a profound indebtedness on the part of Wesley to the exegesis of the early church.

Yet this tradition is not an unmixed blessing. Thus, for example, Wesley's reading of the pericope of the rich young ruler owes more to Clement of Alexandria than it does to an unbiased approach to the New Testament texts themselves. For it was Clement who invented the dodge that the distribution of all possessions to the poor was not a prerequisite for the following of Christ but rather a sort of interior distance from these possessions.[28] In this way Christianity was accommodated to the common sense of the prosperous classes of Alexandria. Thus both at the level of biblical exegesis and at that of a study of the church's reflection on scripture we are confronted with the embodiment of the divine project of justice for the wretched of the earth and with the ways in which that project has been compromised and evaded.

The same will be true of an investigation of the thought of Wesley himself. In my book I indicated some of the ways in which, especially in the middle years of his ministry, Wesley seems to have muted his own convictions concerning economics in the attempt to reduce the scandal of the Methodist project. That is, there are ways in which Wesley himself may have laid the foundation for the failure of the Methodist project to liberate itself from the suffocating restrictions of worldly prudence.[29] But whatever may be alleged concerning this period of Wesley's work it is clear that Methodism after Wesley has been characterized by the headlong rush to abandon Wesley's option for the marginalized. Indeed the study of Wesley has often done more to obscure than to clarify the radicalism of Wesley's views on economic justice. For example, Sugden's notes in *Wesley's Standard Sermons* simply dismiss references by Wesley to the communalism of the primitive church.[30]

The result of this sort of "interpretation" of Wesley has been that Wesley is often portrayed by friends as well as enemies as one who gave religious sanction to the middle-class accommodation to capitalism. If we are to attempt to actualize a Wesleyan and evangelical turn to the poor we must also be historically informed concerning the variety of ways in which such a project can go wrong, can sabotage itself and so render itself ineffective. This holds true not only for the study of Wesley and his interpreters but also for the history of the Methodist movement itself. It is of course important to ransack our collective history for models and examples of a clear and courageous commitment to the poor and oppressed. Fortunately there are illustrations of this in all periods and places of our mission. But it would be disingenuous to suppose that these illustrations of commitment represent a history of noble achievement for the Methodist movement as such. In the first place such movements whether in the abolition of slavery or the organization of workers, or the capacitation of untouchables, or the identification with the aspirations of oppressed peoples in Africa or Asia or Latin America, have regularly been opposed both by the main body of people called Methodist and by those who have held positions of influence or power within the movement.

This is all too easily forgotten in the aftermath of a concrete struggle. We imagine that Methodists have generally opposed slavery or apartheid or imperialism, that Methodists have been on the side of women's rights or civil rights for minorities or excluded majorities. But this is manifestly not the case. We also know that the people called Methodist have collaborated with Apartheid in South Africa, supported slavery in North America, and been tools of Western economic hegemony in the mission movement. Historical inquiry should enable us to identify those strategies by which we have again and again persuaded ourselves to collaborate with the principalities and powers of domination and division.[31]

If we are to produce a usable history of the people called Meth-

36

odists, we must not engage in illusion, for it is the truth alone that can make us free from the patterns of the past. Put another way, it is only through the clear confession of sin that we approach that grace that is capable of saving us not only from the guilt but also the power of sin, that can liberate us from the compulsion to repeat the errors of the past. This is but an outline of the agenda that faces us. It is a formidable task that awaits us, and only by the energizing and transforming power of God's grace will we be able to address it. But nothing less would be worthy of the people called Methodists.

As the bearers of Methodist tradition and the representatives of Methodist institutions we may find ourselves falling under the curse of Wesley. This is what he wrote two and a half centuries ago:

> Lay this deeply to heart, ye who are now a poor, despised, afflicted people. Hitherto ye are not able to relieve your own poor. But if ever your substance increase, see that ye be not straightened in your bowels, that ye fall not into the same snare of the devil. Before any of you either lay up treasures on earth, or indulge needless expenses of any kind, I pray the Lord God to scatter you to the corners of the earth, and blot out your name from under heaven![32]

It is my earnest hope that we will find a way to rescue the people called Methodists from the curse of Wesley and enable this people to be again the embodiment of the promise of Methodism, so that it may be true also for us that:

> Never in any age or nation, since the age of the Apostles, have these words been so eminently fulfilled, "The poor have the gospel preached to them," as it is at this day.[33]

37

CHAPTER 2

Good News for the Poor:
A Black African Biblical Hermeneutics

ITUMELENG MOSALA

Editor's Note: In the summer of 1992, when this essay was written, the political situation in South Africa was vastly different than it is today. Because the author's concern was in large measure to demonstrate the importance of reading the Bible from particular social locations, the essay has been left in its original form.

Introduction

Naming ourselves is a matter that cannot be entered into carelessly. I use the terms black African in a very specific way. Being a South African allows one the privilege of being either an African or a black, or as in my case a black African. In the volatile and dangerous political situation of the past twenty years in South Africa these identities have sometimes carried deadly implications.

To understand these identities and the differences between them is to understand key distinctions not only in politics, but even in ecclesiology and spiritual praxis such that a Christian statesperson of the calibre and integrity of the Presiding Bishop of the Methodist Church, Stanley Mmutlanyane Mogoba, and Frank Chikane of the South African Council of Churches are forced to be on different, if not opposing, sides. Similarly three Methodists at the head of three of the major black political organizations in South Africa do not only differ in perspectives and ideology, but are dangerously poised possibly to lead millions into a potentially catastrophic conflict with one another. I refer here to Nelson Mandela for the African National Congress (ANC); to the highly regarded Methodist preacher and founder/leader of the Pan Africanist Congress (PAC), the late Robert Mangaliso Sobukwe; and, to myself, for the Azanian People's Organization (AZAPO), the political organization started by Steve Biko, himself killed by the South Africans in 1977.

Critically, for my purposes here, these identities frame the way in which the Bible has been read, is being read, and can be read in the South African situation. To be an African, therefore, is to be connected to the land of Africa, the histories of the people of Africa, and the culture and spiritualities of the people of Africa. To be black is to know and consciously and deliberately embody the political implications of being African. The implications for a biblical hermeneutics of liberation are enormous.

As the recent history of South Africa has shown, one can also be other things. For example, one can be non-racial. This is a different identity which has its own implications for reading the Bible. The biblical hermeneutics of the Kairos document emanates from this identity. This explains the difficulties that Kairos theologians had in making the Kairos document an African or a black document. Its impact was more among non-blacks and non-Africans than among blacks and Africans in South Africa.

Context

The starting point of a black biblical hermeneutics of liberation is the historical, social, economic, cultural, and political texts of black people. We exist, therefore we read. Our existence, however, is not monolithic. For this reason, we must expand our hermeneutic to state that we read in order to exist. Reading the Bible is a thoroughly political act in our case, as indeed in any case anywhere, appearances notwithstanding. The difference is that we choose to engage this fact deliberately.

The key hermeneutical question facing those who look to the Bible for the liberation of their humanity is not whether or not they read, but what they are reading and with whose eyes they are reading. The eyes of the poor have yet to read the Bible. For without this new presence of the poor in the business of reading the Bible, there is no recovering the erstwhile presence of the poor in the stories of the Bible.

Thus in seeking to develop a hermeneutic of good news to the poor in South Africa the question is no longer on which side God is.

40

That was a good question for its time. Now, however, the relevant question is how to interpret the eloquence with which the poor are silent and the absence through which they are present in the pages of the Bible. It is in struggling with these silences and absences that a new and creative reappropriation of the liberation of the gospel takes place. It would be nice to know that God is on our side, but in the context of the South African reality we simply cannot start there.

It is as well to point out already that this biblical hermeneutical perspective raises serious questions concerning the Wesleyan doctrinal emphasis on assurance. What does it really mean for black South African Christians to know that they are saved by faith through grace? Again the issue is not that they would not like to be, but exactly what does it amount to affirm such a faith? But let us first turn to our biblical hermeneutical struggles. I will focus on a reading of Exodus 1–2 in order to highlight the issues at stake for a black hermeneutics of liberation.

Exodus 1–2: Some Hermeneutical Reflections

It is common knowledge that oppressed peoples who share the Christian faith have found great inspiration in the exodus story of the liberation of slaves from bondage. It is also common knowledge that the same story has provided arsenal and justification for the colonization of black people and other oppressed peoples by white people. It is now becoming common knowledge that some white people no longer shy away from defending the "unusability" of the exodus story for liberation purposes. The prime example of this latter position is the review two years ago of Jorge Pixley's commentary on Exodus by John Levenson.[1]

The debate about whether Exodus should or should not be used in this way, and who has the right to determine so, is not part of my concern here. Rather, I seek to ask (like Renita Weems, to whom I am indebted in this essay, and Allen Warrior, with whom I share many sentiments) whether Exodus can really and genuinely be liberating for native peoples—Africans, Americans, Aboriginals, Maoris, etc.—and what Methodism has to do with or to say to this? The other issue à la Levenson, whether oppressed peoples have a right to use the exodus for political purposes, does not require the permission of white people or, what amounts to the same thing, the permission of the biblical scholarly guild.

41

Crucial for the struggles for human liberation is the ability of the story and text of Exodus, especially when taken in its entirety, to deliver the goods to the dispossessed majority of the world's population. Renita Weems concludes her illuminating study of the way in which the ideology of difference in the text of Exodus 1 structures race, gender, and sexual relations by asking and replying: "Can those involved in race, gender, and/or class struggles in modern society use this story as a positive example in their struggle for liberation? Not without due caution."[2] I have been of the same view for some while on the basis of the nature and history of the text, not to say anything about the ideological practices inscribed in it, as Weems points out so clearly. The most recent confirmation from traditional biblical scholarship which points in this direction, albeit unintentionally, is the conclusion of John van Seters that Exodus 1–2 represents Yahwistic historiographical imaginativeness and inventiveness. According to van Seters, the Yahwist who produced Exodus 1–2 is not reliant upon an ancient stratum of tradition. On the contrary, the Yahwist uses elements from the account of Solomon's reign, but is not for that reason contemporaneous with the period from which those elements come. He emphasizes that

> . . . it is Dtr's understanding of the time of Solomon that is reflected in J's use of this material. This historiographic presentation of the sojourn in Egypt must therefore be post-Dtr. It goes without saying that it can hardly yield any useful information about the date or circumstances of an Egyptian sojourn and efforts to correlate it with elements from Egyptian historical sources are a waste of time.[3]

There are far-reaching hermeneutical implications in the fact, if indeed it is a fact, that certain parts of the exodus story are Solomonic or at least monarchic. The key hermeneutical question, therefore, is not, as the likes of Levenson have implied, simply whether Exodus should be used for liberation purposes. More fundamentally the question is what results are possible when Exodus is used, whether by protagonists of liberation or by beneficiaries of the status quo. From the South African perspective the question has gone beyond the liberal preoccupation with who has the right to use the Exodus, the white apartheid state or black oppressed masses. The real question is what is in Exodus that seems to make it more effective as a tool of colonization and oppression than as an instrument of liberation. Black biblical hermeneutics has gone beyond moralistic condemnation of the apartheid state for "misusing" the Exodus story. The task of a black biblical hermeneutics of liberation is to find out whether the text of the bible itself is open to use in the way in which colonizers have used it, and if so, why.

This takes us back to the Solomonic or monarchic character of Exodus 1–2. I should add that the text need not have been monarchic simply by virtue of its monarchic provenance. However, the question of the class character of the story of the midwives and Moses is a relevant one. It places the liberation of the slaves from bondage in Egypt under a different light. The issue is no longer how a population of slaves struggles to find freedom from a slave holding nation, but how a story about the liberation of slaves fares in the hands of those who write for a state that itself is engaged in slave labor, land dispossession of peasants, and a program of imperialist annexation of other people's lands.

Seen from this perspective, the political contradiction at the heart of the exodus story takes on a different complexion. I refer here to the inherent contradiction of a story of liberation from slavery for the purpose of taking over the land of the Palestinians, all in the name of God, and in the name of the chosenness of the colonizing nation. This contradiction is less God's contradiction, which in the nature of theology is anyway non-contradictory, than the contradiction born of the workings of hegemonic ideology. The exodus story is a coopted story. Both Moses and the midwives must be reevaluated in the light of this observation.

The disjunction between liberation and colonization in Exodus happens in the text before it happens in situations where Exodus is used, like South Africa. The contextualization of the exodus story by different political and ideological generations of Israelite people itself means that the concerns and commitments of these generations became the concerns and commitments of the canonical text of Exodus.

Beyond the Midwives and the Princess

It is often very tempting for oppressed communities to seek to find themselves in every text of the Bible. Hence certain forms of black theology and feminist theology have attempted to reclaim certain characters and stories for themselves. The actions of the midwives in Exodus provide precisely this temptation. The story makes them out to be heroines who use their professional role to support the resistance and survival of an enslaved community. I have already pointed out that Renita Weems sees a basic inadequacy in the failure of this story to question the ideology of difference that is used to explain one of the contradictions of the situation.

In addition to this key issue of difference between the Hebrew women and the Egyptian women we also need to ask who these women are anyway. Is it enough that they are Shiprah and Puah? How are they related to Pharaoh, or shall we say Solomon? Are they liberating figures in the way in which they are presented? If the exodus had not been influenced by the Solomonic context in the way in which it was, would the descendants of the exodus slaves have produced this account of the resistance against Pharaoh? What is the logic that keeps the mothers of those who were born under the circumstances described silent? The privileging of the Princess over against the slave mothers in the story certainly points to class interests and class commitments on the part of this Solomonic, yet post-Deuteronomist, text that cannot be speaking of the liberation of slaves? Is it possible that instead we are dealing here with the liberation of the Israelite state from domination by other imperial powers? How else is one to read the political significance of 1:9 ("Look, the Israelite people are more numerous and more powerful than we are") and 1:20-21 ("So God dealt well with the midwives; and the people multiplied and became very strong. And because the midwives feared God, he gave them families of their own") which scholars have already pointed out are of a kind with promises to the patriarchs in Genesis? And do we not know that those promises refer to realities that happened under the Davidic imperial expansion? This should surely explain the ideology of difference which Renita Weems has identified as hermeneutically problematic in a story about liberation.

Beyond Moses and Pharaoh

Apart from its anti-African ethos, the story of Moses and the dynamics surrounding him and Pharaoh presents a difficulty for a hermeneutics of liberation. A key element of the problem is the silence of the slaves. This, however, is unavoidable, given the entirely ruling-class context of Moses' rebellion. The story is undoubtedly moving as an account of survival and rebellion on the part of someone who could have remained comfortable. But is it the kind of story of one who underpinned by an ideology as a comfortable, unoppressed person becomes the hero of the uncomfortable and oppressed people?

Again, it is the silence of the slaves which is hermeneutically disturbing. It is also the sociological distance. Moses *goes out* to *visit* his people. The next day he *went back*. He kills the Egyptian *on behalf of* the slave workers! And then he expects them to trust and believe him when he utters that familiar blacker-than-thou political self-righteousness: "Why are you beating up a fellow-Hebrew?"

Indeed the slaves do speak! But they speak in tongues they are not expected to. There is no mistaking the text's disapproval of what the slaves say: "Who made you a ruler and judge over us? Do you mean to kill me as you killed the Egyptian?" (Exod 2:14). I can hear Moses and those who share his class and ideological commitments murmur in their hearts angrily: "You fool, don't you know I am on your side, not on my side?" So Moses does have a side other than that of the slaves, only he does not choose it.

In order not to choose his side, therefore, Moses must talk with Pharaoh to *negotiate* the freedom of the slaves. By this time of course the slaves are not only silenced, they are absent. What needs to be kept in mind, though, is that this is not really surprising. This post-deuteronomistic story of the Solomonic state is not about the liberation of slaves. On the contrary, it seeks to harness the full ideological potential of the state to explain why the land of the Canaanites has justifiably been annexed and why the genocidal slaughter of the people of the land was only part of the divine plan. The story of exodus makes absolute ruling-class sense. It is only when an attempt is made to appropriate it as an oppressed people's story that the contradictions emerge. As it stands, the contradictions are an inherent part of it.

Liberating the Text

The text of Exodus no longer belongs to the slaves. In this regard, though, it joins to form a part of an imposing majority in the Bible. The history of other stories is the same. The Soviet Union and Eastern Europe notwithstanding, Marx's words continue to ring true even for the exodus: "In every epoch the ruling ideas are the ideas of the ruling class" (German Ideology). It is the liberation not just of the slaves but also of the texts and stories of the slaves that are a condition of the freedom of the slaves. Reading the Bible in the context of the black struggle and in particular of the black-consciousness philosophy in South Africa inexorably points to the importance of the praxis of the slaves and oppressed peoples. Through their praxis against their present enslavement will come the liberation of the stories and texts of slaves. And in a dialectical fashion, only then will the stories themselves be liberating.

Exodus stands in a similar political hermeneutical tradition with Daniel, Esther, Ruth, to name a few in the Hebrew Bible, and with the parables of the gold coins/talents, the vineyard tenants, and the woman who anointed Jesus on the eve of Calvary. It is the silencing of slaves, oppressed peoples, and women that characterizes these texts and the privileging of ruling class perspectives in them which raises hermeneutical problems for us. Whose stories are they?

Needless to say, the cry for the reopening of the canon of scripture in order to liberate its full potential has long been heard among scholars of the oppressed. In the meantime the oppressed people of our time who still rely upon and utilize the resources of scripture for their spirituality have gone ahead and done so through their everyday praxis. But what about the Methodist canon? How have ordinary Methodists fared on issues related to Wesleyan spirituality and its groundedness in the stories of the Bible?

Methodism, the Bible, and Black People

Despite John Wesley, Methodism is of necessity a people's movement. The sociology of its structures and the political economy of its doctrines betray as much. Its weapons of struggle are discursive and cultural in stark contrast to the institutional power of its competitors both at the time of its origin and since. It is a genuinely post-Reformation movement which presupposes the political and economic developments that took place in post feudal Europe. Take away the proletarian masses and it reduces to no more than an attenuated form of its predecessors. Assurance, sanctification, and perfection are the stuff of which people's spiritualities are made. And it is good. But having said this, I must retreat from the "enthusiastic" and "triumphalist" exposition of Wesleyan doctrine against which José Míguez Bonino warns.[4] Its doctrines and social history have, despite itself, been for those of us in the Third World, "part of the history of our

46

domination and exploitation."[5] It shares in the indictment which Sergio Rostagno makes against the church when he declares:

> Historically speaking, the church has always been a church of the bourgeoisie, even when it claimed to transcend class barriers or labored under the illusion that it pervaded all classes in the same way. Indeed, it has been a truly bourgeois church, if the notion of interclassism is taken as part of bourgeois ideology. . . . The church has been the church of the class which has identified itself with the history of the West, in which Christianity may be considered to have been a major force. Only those members of the working class who accepted this view of history attended church. But most of the working people never accepted this view and only gave the church the kind of formal allegiance subjects give to the claims of their rulers. They could not really belong to the church of another class.[6]

And so we move from asking of the texts of liberation in the Bible, Whose texts these are? to asking about the church, Whose church this really is? to asking about Methodism, Whose spirituality are we really dealing with here? Is it any wonder that Methodism prevented a revolution in Britain—a fact of no mean displeasure for those of us attempting to overthrow oppressive regimes?

The doctrines of assurance and perfection are not objectionable. They can hardly be for those groaning under the yoke of economic debt, social alienation, and political dispossession. But are they liberating? Are they more than Exodus and Luke and all those parables that speak for and on behalf of the poor but never really represent the voice of the poor itself, let alone the action of the poor?

Es'kia Mphahlele, a black South African novelist educated at one of Methodism's best institutions, Kilnerton in the Transvaal, returned to South Africa after twenty years of exile to find a political mood and a style such as the one at which Jeremiah's invectives were directed when he said "They have treated the wound of my people carelessly, saying 'Peace, peace,' when there is no peace" (Jer 8:11). In reacting to the optimism and triumphalism which the powers-that-be were creating he focused on a song that the Ministry of Information of the South African government was sponsoring. The title of his article in the black magazine Tribute was: "Whose Song, Whose Peace?" It is this question that frames, relentlessly, the biblical hermeneutic of struggle in South Africa.

When we turn to the fundamental beliefs of Methodism the question stays with us: Whose assurance, whose perfection? A few excerpts from Es'kia Mphahlele's article might give flavor and context to the dilemma of a black Methodist reading the Bible in the 1990s in South Africa. He writes at the beginning of the article: "I wonder why so many people often believe that they can say and do things that hurt millions of other people and then simply make amends with a song that will say soothing words." And then again later: "We all know that the South African Statute Book is the best and most eloquent textbook on racism." Referring to an incident that had just happened between a young white man and a black young woman, Mphahlele continues: "We have witnessed a young man plead guilty to raping and murdering an 18-year-old woman and then cry out, 'God has forgiven me, so man must also forgive me.'" And finally, in a tone that exemplifies the pain of black Christian spirituality and its relation with the Bible on the one hand and Methodist faith on the other hand, Mphahlele writes:

> Amidst all this pain and alienation among the unfree, and the tough and menacing talk among the rulers, the legalized violence that is generated by this class, amidst this whole process that alienates family and community members from one another and from the law and its minions, a song is born that speaks of peace and co-operation in the building of some resplendent future for everyone. The mud house . . . the choir set up by those who have power . . . the oppressed called upon to sing while chafing under the yoke and the cruelty of the times. How cynical, how exasperating![7]

Yet some black people did take part in the singing of the song, albeit at great expense physically for themselves and their families. The reason is that it was done in the name of peace. Who can say after three hundred years of suffering that they do not want peace? But whose peace was it? Indeed, even today whose peace is it? More to today's point: Whose Bible is it? and Whose Methodism is it?

For black people in the Christian fold and in the Methodist tradition the question has been simplified. What does it mean to read the Bible in the aftermath of the Rodney King case in Los Angeles and the murder of black people in Boipatong, South Africa? Is it still possible to be Christian and Methodist after Los Angeles and Boipatong?

CHAPTER 3

The *Imitatio Christi* and the Great Commandment: Virtue and Obligation in Wesley's Ministry with the Poor

RICHARD P. HEITZENRATER

Introduction

About ten years ago, John Walsh asked me a question that has been pricking my mind ever since: Why was Wesley so interested in helping the poor? What was Wesley's motivation for working with the poor?

Of course, the description of Wesley's activities in this regard is rather commonplace. Any list of such activities would certainly include teaching, feeding, and clothing the poor children; furnishing gainful employment to the jobless; giving loans to struggling entre-preneurs; visiting the sick and the prisoners; providing food, cloth-ing, money, shelter, books, medicine, and other essentials to the needy.[1] Yet, let me repeat what is obvious and has been mentioned many times: These were not the normal daily activities expected of an eighteenth-century Oxford don, especially one such as Wesley, who was raised in a relatively posh Church of England rectory by parents with a scholarly bent (even though in the hinterlands), schooled in one of the finest public schools in the country, educated at purportedly the best of the Oxford colleges, and fellow of another college at the University. Nevertheless, such was the case, though it is much easier to describe than to explain Wesley's penchant for helping the poor. We might note in passing that the description itself has often been given through modern eyes that try to present

Wesley's actions in such a manner as to support a given current perspective or program of activity.

We tend to ignore or skip over those aspects of Wesley's thought or action that seem to portray him in ways that are now thought of as outdated, insensitive, shortsighted, or perhaps just plain wrong (or, in any case, embarrassing to us). I'm not quite sure which should be more embarrassing to a present-day historian—to see Wesley twisted into a prototype of a modern perspective that he does not really fit, or to see him portrayed in ways that display his faults and quirks with all their eighteenth-century shortcomings, blemishes, flaws, and imperfections. In any case, to press the question of "Why?" is to go beyond descriptive terms and to ask for an analysis of the motivation that lies behind such an extensive program of activity. With this question in mind, I looked at several recent descriptive portraits of Wesley and the poor, keeping in mind the question, Why?

Wesley and the Poor in Recent Scholarship

Manfred Marquardt, in his *John Wesley's Social Ethics*,[2] represents an expression of the more or less traditional view of Wesley and the poor. Wesley's charitable activities are seen to be part of an ethic of love, based on the Great Commandment—to love God and love neighbor. Such charitable activities are an obedient response to the divine command, the fulfillment of an ethical obligation (p. 33). For Marquardt, again representing well the long tradition of Wesleyan historiography, there is a dynamic shift in the theological underpinning of Wesley's view around 1738. Prior to that (especially while at Oxford), Wesley helped the poor as part of an attempt to do good works in order to earn his salvation, and this effort was part of his self-affirmation before God. The author follows Vulliamy in claiming that Wesley's formal High Church attempt to earn salvation through works-righteousness at Oxford therefore disqualify that period from even being considered as authentically "Methodist," since it was supposedly so entirely foreign to Methodism's real (later) spirit (pp. 26, 145 n. 33). Marquardt (in good continental Reformation perspective) sees Wesley's good works after 1738 flowing forth as a response of faith to God's justifying love (pp. 98–101).

In the midst of his study, Marquardt does provide a basic outline of Wesley's theology, but the radical emphasis on *sola fide* fails to recognize Wesley's mature position (seen in the 1767 sermon, "The

Scripture Way of Salvation") that good works (even before justification) were "in some sense" necessary for salvation.[3] It is interesting also to note that this typical "watershed" interpretation of Wesley's life, bifurcating it into two main sections, before and after Aldersgate, seems to overlook the fact that Wesley's attitude and activities relative to the poor remain remarkably consistent, both before and after 1738. In fact, seeing Wesley's later employment of a charitable program of activities (even in a faithful response to God's love), as done simply in obedience to a command (dominical or otherwise) results in a dynamic that is very close to the sort of legalism or works-righteousness that was worrisome to the Calvinists and Lutherans (and especially to the Moravians) in Wesley's day.

In a more recent work entitled *Good News to the Poor*,[4] Theodore W. Jennings, Jr., comes at Wesley's program from a somewhat different perspective but with some similar assumptions. Jennings sees Wesley's "holiness project" as starting at Oxford with the dedication of all of his resources to the poor on the basis of the clear commands and instructions of the Gospels (especially Matthew 25:40—"just as you did it to one of the least of these who are members of my family, you did it to me"). This implied command represents the sort of obligation that the Christian ought to fulfill (p. 140). Again, the theological context for action is seen by Jennings to be altered in the late 1730s and early 1740s (not strictly speaking in May 1738), so that good works were then to be understood as flowing from grace and no longer entailed an outward correspondence to an external law, but rather a correspondence to the same "law" now internalized. Nevertheless, the dynamic remains much the same: the necessity of following the divine instructions (p. 141).

In a certain sense, therefore, Jennings sees more explicit continuity in the motivation for Wesley's activities with the poor. He goes on to describe Wesley's program of charitable activity primarily in terms of "spreading scriptural holiness," entailing the transformation of individuals and of the economic and political order, "the establishment of pentecostal commun(al)ism, and the abolition of war" (pp. 141–53). In all of this discussion, the theological basis of Wesley's ethic is only outlined in very general terms, and Jennings' comments that purport to present Wesley's views and intentions are often not quite recognizable and often not documented in Wesley's own writings.

Jennings does, however, go beyond the typical "obligation" point of view in noting that Wesley encouraged his preachers to visit the sick, the poor, the prisoners, not simply in obedient fulfillment of a command or obligation, but also in order (by visiting in person) to gain an increase in lowliness (humility), patience, tenderness of spirit, and sympathy—i.e., an increase in virtue. This approach assumes the possibility of acquiring the virtues by the exercise of them. Thus, visiting the poor sick is not only a sign of virtue, but also a means of acquiring virtue (pp. 54, 57–58). Jennings, in passing, notes (though does not emphasize) an important point: that Wesley saw Jesus as both the model and as the empowerment for this activity: "Go and see the poor in their hovels [as Wesley told Miss March in June 1775], . . . Jesus went before you and will go with you."[5]

What is not evident in Jennings' claim of Wesley's "preferential option for the poor" is the fact that the poor of which Wesley spoke were not "them" but "us." The "poor of the Society," to use Wesley's common phrase,[6] were not outsiders who were the occasional object of his external social outreach—they were, by and large, the people who made up a relatively large proportion of his societies and for whom he and the Methodists had specific pastoral responsibility. The point is a major one that Jennings by and large misses—the issue has not so much to do with the nature of the church's mission to the larger society; rather, the issue has to do with the nature of the church itself.

Henry Abelove's recent biography of Wesley, entitled *The Evangelist of Desire*,[7] tries to deal with many of the same questions and themes as Marquardt and Jennings, especially Wesley's relationship to the poor (or "the plebeians," in Abelove's terminology), but his work differs starkly in many of its assumptions and conclusions. We cannot hope for much help from Abelove in matters of Wesley's theology—he excuses himself from the discussion by claiming that Wesley "taught the Methodists no particular theology" (p. 74). The short chapter on "Spirituality" does not provide any hint as to the connection between the basic Wesleyan soteriology and the ethics of one's daily actions. But the latter are seen rather consistently in terms of instructions, injunctions, demands, prohibitions, and rules, all of which represent the obligation perspective in its starkest form.[8]

The "ethic of love," however, takes on an odd new twist in this study. Abelove claims that, on the one hand, Wesley "played the gentleman and exacted deference" from his people (consisting largely of the poor), and on the other hand he "won and monopolized love." This love secured the deference, together providing a "seductive and monopolistic" approach that was uniquely successful in managing the plebeians (again, read "poor") that comprised the movement (pp. xii, 6–7, 24). Abelove is at least aware (*contra* Jennings) that Wesley's "preferential option" was first for his own people (those of the household of faith, to use one of Wesley's favorite scriptural phrases), who for the most part were poor (pp. 27–28). This fact can be demonstrated specifically by Wesley's own comments about such activities as his medical clinic.[9] Only within such a context can one understand how Wesley could propose a community of goods—a common store of goods has a chance of working within a group that falls within a relatively narrow band on the economic spectrum. Any wider disparity and gaps in economic level would have allowed serious discussion only of charity and philanthropy, not communalism.

In Abelove's view, however, Wesley was so successful in his contriving to win the love of his flock, that he had to worry (a tad, at least) about whether he was competing too successfully with God as the object of the peoples' affection (p. 37). And part of Wesley's charitable scheme, according to Abelove, was the unique combination of offering salvation to the poor in addition to offering them monetary and physical assistance (p. 31; I have never before seen Wesley's soteriology categorized under "charity"). Wesley's "success" as defined by Abelove is just as implausible as Wesley's "failure" as defined by Jennings.

One thing that can be said for Abelove, however, is that he does delve into a fascinating selection of contemporary diaries and letters from the eighteenth century in trying to answer an important question—What did the Methodist people themselves think and do in the light of Wesley's teachings and actions? (pp. 58, 107–9). The point is that we should not assume that there is a necessary correlation between Wesley's ideas and actions and those of his people. As we know, the people did not always (in some cases, not often) do what Wesley suggested or think as Wesley thought. For instance, apparently only one in a hundred, at best, followed his third rule on the use of money (give all you can). It is the type of question that is difficult to trace fully or document extensively, but should always be kept in mind when we talk about Wesley and eighteenth-century Methodism.

John Walsh's brilliant discussion of "John Wesley and the Community of Goods"[10] is especially intriguing because of his references to a variety of places where Wesley talks about the Christian life in terms of precedents and models. Walsh notes that Wesley suggested, quite early on, that Christians of his day might live, as well as believe, as did the Primitive Christians (pp. 29–30). Following the lead of Clement of Alexandria, Wesley depicts the ideal Christian in his outline of "The Character of a Methodist" (1742), again providing a model for all to follow, that model being defined in terms of a person who has the distinguishing marks of the genuine Christian, one who "loves God" and "loves his neighbor." Walsh also points out that Wesley is convinced that the spirit of preaching that urged virtues upon the early Christians should elicit a similar response in his own day (p. 30–31).

In a particularly important observation, Walsh provides a clue to the answer for the question, Why did Wesley work with the poor? He points out that Wesley says charity is not a series of episodic acts but a way of life (p. 35). For Wesley, then, the Christian life is not defined primarily by *doing* certain activities but by *being* a certain kind of person. In terms of ethical theory, virtue ethics, for Wesley, is more basic than obligation ethics, though they necessarily interrelate and correlate. Virtue takes precedence over obedience; "being" has priority over "doing."

Virtue and Obligation Ethics

Professor Frederick S. Carney claims that three approaches constitute the entire range of normative elements available to anyone's ethic: obligation, virtue, and value.[11] A brief summary his description of these three approaches follows:

(1) *Obligation Theory* answers the question, What ought to be done? What actions are appropriate?
 • Decisions are framed within the options of right or wrong actions, norms, or policies.
 • This approach uses principles, rules, commands, and standards to guide the decisions.
 • Failure, in this mode, is seen in terms of the guilt of violation, transgression, or omission.
 • Such failure can be overcome by accepting forgiveness for wrong actions.

(2) *Virtue Theory* answers the question, What kind of person should I be? What sort of character is most appropriate?
- Decisions are framed in terms of good or bad qualities, dispositions, motives, and actions.
- This approach uses models, portrayals of the ideal, of what is just or good.
- Failure, in this mode, is seen in terms of shame of weakness.
- Such failure can be overcome by the experience of transformation (rebirth or new life).

(3) *Value Theory* answers the question, What objects or states of affairs are important (or more important than others)?
- Decisions are framed within a range of good or bad objects or states of affairs.
- This approach uses sets, scales, or grades of good and evil.
- Failure, in this mode, is seen in terms of remorse for accepting false or over-valued ideals, idols.
- Such failure can be overcome by a reorientation of the operative value system.

For our purposes in examining Wesley's activities, the nature of and interrelationship between the first two approaches, virtue and obligation, are especially important. Another significant element in this ethical analysis, as pointed out by Carney, is the role of truth. To make a long story short, truth is joined with love to form the basic principle of Wesley's theological ethic. Benevolence (love of neighbor) is no virtue at all unless it springs from the love of God.[12] And at the same time, Wesley is constantly admonishing his hearers to "speak the truth in love" (Eph 4:15). As Wesley goes on to say,

> This then is real, genuine, solid virtue. Not truth alone, nor simply conformity to truth. That is a *property* of real virtue, not the *essence* of it. Nor is it love alone, though this comes nearer the mark; for 'love' in one sense 'is the fulfilling of the law'. No: truth and love united together are the essence of virtue or holiness.[13]

Virtue in Wesley's Theological Ethics

To see how such a theological ethic of virtue works throughout the teaching and ministry of Wesley, let us first remember that his soteriology from the beginning comes to a practical focus on the doctrine of sanctification. Let us also recall his constant reiteration of the three grand themes that comprise Methodist teaching, as he said in the 1740s and was wont to point out to the Anglican clergy in the 1750s and 1760s:

> Our main doctrines, which include all the rest, are three, that of repentance, of faith, and of holiness. The first of these we account, as it were, the porch of religion, the next, the door; the third, religion itself.[14]

As Wesley indicated, these three terms imply a variety of other terms, which he uses in a number of ways on various occasions, such as original sin, justification, sanctification. Nevertheless, holiness, or sanctification, is the crux of what he will often refer to as true religion, or religion itself. In spite of an obvious tendency toward synergism in much of his thinking, holiness, for Wesley, does not refer primarily to the results of human effort seen in a set of acts or activities, but rather to the renewal of human nature in reference to an ideal.

This perspective was as evident for Wesley in 1733 as it was in 1791. Salvation is not effected through effort or activity; Christian perfection is not a collection of perfect acts. In his sermon on "Circumcision of the Heart," he points out that holiness implies being cleansed from sin and, by consequence, "being endued with those virtues which were also in Christ Jesus, the being so 'renewed in the image of our mind' as to be 'perfect, as our Father in heaven is perfect'."[15] In Athanasius' terms, we are "to become by grace what God is by nature."

One of Wesley's most constant concerns (as indicated by the prolific references to it in Wesley's earliest diary at Oxford, beginning in 1725), was inward: "purity of intention." Another of his convictions, again from the 1720s, was of the absolute necessity of God's grace in the drama of salvation. The theme of prevenient grace is evident in his diaries in the early 1730s. And the focus of the Methodist scheme of devotion during the Oxford period was, as I have pointed out before, a form of meditative piety that focused on the virtues, implanted by grace.[16]

Virtue, for Wesley, was the wellspring of the holy life. Self-examination was a means to self-knowledge, and the Oxford Methodists carried out a "particular examination" of themselves every day, using a list of questions based on the traditional list of virtues for each day of the week:

Sunday	Love of God
Monday	Love of Man [neighbor]

Tuesday	Humility
Wednesday	Mortification and self-denial
Thursday	Resignation and meekness
Friday	Mortification and self-denial
Saturday	Thankfulness

The purpose of their self-examination was to become aware of specific sins and to plant in their place the corresponding virtue. This process was not so much dependent upon rules that demanded obedience (obligation ethic); the emphasis was not on the performance of certain good works. Rather, the questions were designed to examine one's actions as a measure of the development of virtue and thus to gauge the inclination of one's heart and affections, an unfailingly inward focus, and a process that Wesley acknowledged (as we have noted) was absolutely dependent upon God's grace.[17] Many of their eighteenth-century colleagues did not understand or appreciate the inward motivation and dynamic that elicited their visible and public program of activity; some saw them as exhibiting "enthusiastic madness and superstitious scruples"[18] The same has been true of many subsequent interpreters. Nineteenth-century evangelicals saw them as (at best) well-intentioned Pharisees who had not yet seen the light (or felt its warmth). And twentieth-century commentators are often no better at careful analysis of the Oxford Methodists. But their activities were of a piece with their theology, which was by no means works-righteousness nor enthusiasm. To understand their activities and lifestyle, one must have a clear grasp of the theological impulses from which those activities sprang.

Oxford Methodist Theology and Ethics

The Oxford "Methodist" lifestyle (often typified as living by method and rule) is perhaps better characterized as meditative piety. If not fully solifidian, it was at least a theology of grace. Benjamin Ingham clearly expressed this side of their soteriological focus in his diary entry of January 31, 1734, when he resolved "God's grace assisting me, to make the salvation of my soul my chief and only concern, but never to depend upon my own strength because I can do nothing without God's assistance."[19] Wesley's sermon of that year, "The One Thing Needful" (Luke 10:42), was already stressing a theme distinctively central to Methodist theology—the necessity to

57

be born again, to be formed anew after the likeness of our Creator, by the agency of the Holy Spirit. This sermon was preached many times by both John and Charles Wesley (yes, the same sermon), both before and after 1738 (this text used over fifty times by John up to 1790).[20] One point that is not often recognized is that most of the early Wesleyan theology was easily woven into his mature theology.

But what about faith? It is there very early as well, in the 1734 manuscript sermon, "The One Thing Needful," where Wesley says that the restoration of the image of God is only effected when the believer has faith, a faith that works in love and draws the person closer toward unity with God, that is, having the mind of Christ and walking as he walked.[21] This last phrase, a conflation of Philippians 2:5 and 1 John 2:6, becomes the central image in his lifelong attempt to define the true Christian; it becomes the most common way of expressing the nature of Christian perfection; it is the most repeated biblical phrase (over fifty references) in his published sermons.[22]

The idea of imitating Jesus, the great Exemplar who "went about doing good" (Acts 10:38), is not only the primary motivation of Wesley's social ethic at Oxford, it is a central and persistent theme throughout his ministry. See, for instance, his later sermon "On Visiting the Sick" (1786), where he talks to the "poor disciples of a poor Master" and encourages them (if not able to give up conveniences or necessities in order to provide for their neighbors necessities or extremities), at least to administer to them the grace of God by doing as Christ did—"whenever thou hast an opportunity, go about doing good, and healing all that are oppressed with the devil."[23] See also his sermon, "The Reward of Righteousness" (1777), where he says,

> To you who believe the Christian revelation, I may speak in a still stronger manner. You believe your blessed Master 'left you an example, that you might tread in his steps' (1 Peter 2:21). Now you know his whole life was a labour of love. You know how he 'went about doing good.'[24]

And to Miss March, whom he is continuing to press on this matter, Wesley explains how his own preferential option for the rich is superseded by the necessity to imitate Christ: given his "druthers," he would like to speak only with the genteel and elegant people; but he can discover no precedent for that in the life of Christ (or of his Apostles). Therefore, he tells her, "let you and I walk as He walked."[25]

In these and many other examples, we can see Wesley's consistent combination of *sola scriptura* and the *imitatio Christi*. And as Ted Jennings has pointed out, Wesley saw Christ not only as the model but as a source of empowerment: "Go and see the poor in their hovels . . . Jesus went before you and will go with you." Wesley's constant stress on the work of the Holy Spirit, the role of faith, and the necessity of grace, means that from the beginning he understood that the Christian's charitable acts are therefore not self-initiated but the result of God's grace. At the same time, full salvation was not viewed as a momentary event so much as a process of restoration and becoming holy. His emphasis was on sanctification, as one presses on, with the assistance of God's grace, toward perfection in love and final salvation. This part of Wesley's message does not change, though between 1737–1740 the place of faith is heightened, its nature is somewhat altered, and the role of justification is clarified.

True religion, for the Oxford Methodists, was not basically a collection of actions that were determined by obedience to various sets of rules. It was conformity to a model: Thomas à Kempis' *De imitatione Christi*, one of the first books in a crucial series of readings for Wesley in the mid-1720s, became the cornerstone of his ethical approach and established the perspective for much of his later thinking on the Christian life. As Wesley said in 1733, the distinguishing mark of a true follower of Christ is nothing outward, but rather inward—"an habitual disposition of the soul"—"a mind and spirit renewed after the image of him that created it."[26] In a later sermon, on "The Way to the Kingdom," he also says, true religion is not to be found in any outward thing, but in the heart, in holiness and happiness, found in love of God and neighbor.[27] In a sermon from 1789, we find him again saying, true religion is right tempers, which he then defines in terms of love of God and neighbor.[28]

It is not an act, then, or a set of acts that defines the Christian. Neither is it obedience to divine commands or conformity to sets of rules. In fact, Wesley points out that a person may feed the hungry or clothe the naked and still have no religion at all.[29] Even love itself is not the simple key, since one might do such acts out of love of praise rather than love of God or neighbor. The love of God, Wesley says, is the "essence, the spirit, the life of all virtue."[30]

Areas of Theological and Ethical Continuity

Perfection, or perfect love, for Wesley, must be understood not as a goal attained through the accumulation of good works or perfect obedience to a particular standard of conduct. Rather, to see it in the context of a virtue-oriented ethic, it is growing conformity to a model of divine-oriented virtue. The goal is not to *act* perfectly; the goal is to *be* perfect, to be open to an inward perfection of intentions and attitudes. Good works are the result of inward dispositions of the soul (virtues), not conformity to particular rules or the accumulation of credit for perfect acts. The Christian life involves a life of devotion that will cultivate these virtues (the imitation of Christ) as well as contend with the concomitant vices (the spiritual combat). The means by which this double-edged form of spirituality could be promoted in the life of the believer were the practices of prayer and meditation.

For Wesley (even at Oxford), good works were not a means to anything, but rather a manifestation of the virtues, the indication of holy tempers (by which Wesley defines "true religion"). Wesley saw this religion exemplified not only in Christ but in the lives of many other persons whom the Methodists considered to have epitomized the Christ-like life. He discovered many of their biographies and writings while he was at Oxford, but published most of them later during the revival—for instance, those of Monsieur deRenty (1741), of Gregory Lopez (1750?), of Madame Guion (1776), and a long series of witnesses to the love of God in the lives of human beings, from Ephraem Syrus and Augustine to Ambrose Bonwicke and James Bonnell.[31]

For Wesley, then, the gospel was simple, epitomized by and aimed at Christian perfection, which Wesley was prone to define (throughout his lifetime) in terms of "having the mind of Christ and walking as he walked." The Christian life is the Christ-like life; a Christian is defined by being, not doing. One cannot really love unless one is loving—one cannot imperatively command patience, or faith, or love—they must be elicited, encouraged, empowered. The life of the faithful Christian is a grace-full life, one that is transformed through the work of Christ, is empowered by the work of the Holy Spirit. It is a life that cultivates the virtues through the practice of meditation, self-examination, and prayer, and manifests its inner reorientation in a disciplined life of devotion and charitable activities. Wesley combines devotional contemplation with acts of charity, links a theology of grace with ethical responsibility, and ties virtue to faith ("faith working through love"), in such a way as to yield a special blend of disciplined devotion and practical piety that gave continuing shape to the Methodist pattern of life and thought.

The understanding of obligation, of course, continues to perform an important role in the Wesleyan ethic, but is subservient to the more basic role of virtue. As such, the obligation aspect of ethics is infused with a different spirit than if it were standing alone as a parallel or alternative approach. And some ethical principles that bear the appearance of having an obligation approach might be reconsidered in the light of these distinctions. One of the most difficult, in this regard, is the Great Commandment itself, to love God and neighbor. The difficulty arises in trying to conceive of love as being obligatory or as being commanded. Virtues cannot be commanded, as we have noted, but must be elicited, or imitated, or implanted. Though the command to love has the form of an obligation ethic, love cannot truly be exercised by anyone who is not a loving person. In this sense, even if love could be considered in obligation terms (doing acts of love), it would need to be preceded by a consideration of virtue (being a loving person).

Another factor that needs more consideration is the matter of the agency of Holy Spirit, and the role of grace and faith. Although Wesley does admit some possibility of acquiring virtues by practice (an acquiremental perspective), his view is basically relational—one becomes good by acceptance within given relationships.[32] Faith does play a role in this process, but not necessarily the precise role that Reformed theology would seem to require. For although the Wesley of the late 1730s and early 1740s says that no good works can take place before justification, both the early Wesley and the mature Wesley allow for just such a possibility.[33] This position is what got him in trouble with Whitefield, with the Moravians, with the Calvinists, and with some of his own Methodists.

In his correspondence with John Smith in the mid 1740s, the problems of the more radical Protestant approach held by Wesley at that time are pointed out to him in very personal terms: if justification requires both a proper faith and a perceptible assurance, and is necessary before any works of devotion or mercy can be considered "good" (and in fact are otherwise works to one's damnation), then by their own testimony in the early 1740s, the Wesleys would have gone to hell if they had died while at Oxford, and their father, Samuel, would have also faced the same predicament. Wesley's careful response began the process of distancing himself from the absolute necessity of assurance and from the denigration of good works prior to justification.[34] Within twenty years, he was, in fact, proclaiming the necessity of good works for salvation, even good works prior to justification, if given the time and opportunity.[34] Although this definitely qualifies any claim that Wesley (after 1738) saw justifying faith as necessarily prerequisite to good works, we must say that Wesley does generally tie faith and love together in talking about such matters. "Faith working through love" is one of his most repeated phrases.

Many of these theological considerations point out that various implications of Wesley's work with the poor are among the several important areas of thought and life in which the stereotypical view of "Aldersgate as watershed" does not fit well (sharp contrast before and after). In the case of Wesley's work with the poor, the activities at Oxford and their theological rationale were in many ways paradigmatic for the theological ethics and charitable activities evident during the rest of his life.[36] In considering the whole area of Wesley's work with the poor, as well as the activities of Oxford Methodism in particular, it is valuable to examine the relationship between theology and ethics, with a particular view to the nature of virtue and obligation ethics, in order to understand more fully what was motivating Wesley in this respect. The old claims about the young Wesley promoting works-righteousness will simply not hold water any more, especially when viewed from the perspective of the whole of Wesley's life and thought.

Conclusion

In summary, I believe that looking at Wesley's work with the poor from the point of view of the important interrelationship between virtue ethics and obligation ethics helps us to understand better several important elements of Wesley's life and thought:

- that a virtue ethic was central to his understanding of the nature of the Christian and the shape of the Christian life;

- that a virtue ethic was quite consistently central to his thinking throughout his life;

- that an obligation ethic was important as a means of fleshing out and measuring the manifestations of virtue in particular areas of endeavor;

- that this significant but subsidiary role of the obligation ethic (seen in rules and works) was misunderstood by Calvinist and Moravian detractors as works-righteousness;

- that the centrality of virtue theory in Wesley's thinking is closely related to his doctrine of sanctification (renewal, becoming holy); and

- that the relationship between virtue theory and obligation theory is important to a fuller understanding of how Wesley's emphasis on "having the mind of Christ and walking as he walked" correlates with the great commandment, "to love God and to love neighbor."

The simple answer, then, to the question, Why did Wesley work with the poor? is, first and foremost, because Jesus did so, but also because Jesus told him to do so and would help him to do so. Renewal in the image of God entails being drawn into God's likeness, as seen in Christ—having the mind of Christ and walking as he walked. If we accept God's truth revealed to us in Christ, we do not have to ask why Christ commanded us to feed the hungry, visit the sick, and clothe the naked, nor do we have to ask why Christ fed the hungry, visited the sick, or clothed the naked; we just need to do it, in faith and in love.

CHAPTER 4

"Good News to the Poor": The Methodist Experience After Wesley

DONALD W. DAYTON

"'To the poor the gospel is preached'—Which is the greatest mercy, and the greatest miracle of all" (John Wesley, *Explanatory Notes on the New Testament*, commenting on the last phrase of Luke 7:22).

Introduction

In this essay I am taking on the nearly impossible task of tracing the theme "Good News to the Poor" through the "post-Wesley" history of the "Methodist" experience, including the great variety of Methodist traditions that derive from Wesley and now cluster themselves together in the World Methodist Council. I will be able to do this in the space available only by severe restrictions. I have chosen a more "cosmic" and illustrative, rather than detailed and comprehensive, method that will result in a more "broad stroke" analysis and interpretation.

I propose to deal with the topic in several steps. First, I will summarize my own reading of the theme in Wesley. Second, I will suggest that the theme "Good News to the Poor" provides a window of access into the very soul of Methodism as it struggles with an ambiguous legacy from Wesley—one in which the Methodist traditions are caught in a profoundly contradictory dialectic of countervailing forces. Third, though it has not often been so used, I will argue that the theme (and its explication in this manner) provides a "hermeneutical key" for a re-reading (*relectura*) of the Methodist tradition—a reading that we must confront more directly than we have generally done in our historical and theological work. Fourth, I will explore the manifestation of this theme in several key "flash-points" of the larger Methodist tradition. And, finally, I will attempt a few closing observations.

It is, of course, "liberation theology," in its various manifestations but most particularly in its South American versions, that has taught the modern church to reflect on a dimension of "divine partiality," that is, the claim that the biblical witness clearly reveals a sort of "preferential option for the poor" that must be taken as an essential and not accidental aspect of the Gospel. The expression is modern, deriving from the title of one of the most controversial documents from the 1979 Puebla (Mexico) meeting of the Latin American Bishops' Conference (CELAM). This origin of the expression means that it often carries today a certain ideological and political freight that obscures the extent to which the basic question it raises has recurred again and again in the history of the church in a variety of ecclesiastical and cultural contexts. Indeed, Justo González has sought roots and antecedents of the idea in the early church and in the resistance to the "colonization" of South America in the wake of Columbus.[1] A forthcoming volume explores the parallels between liberation theology and a variety of nineteenth century radical protestant movements that had each articulated this theme in its own way.[2] In our own time the theme has found expression in such diverse locations as the "sectarian" ethics and theology of Mennonite John Howard Yoder (e. g., his *The Politics of Jesus*, which explores the biblical basis of this theme in the Gospel of Luke) and the "evangelical" social activism of Ronald J. Sider (e.g., *Rich Christians in an Age of Hunger: A Biblical Study*). When I use the expression "preferential option for the poor," I have a more general concept in mind than some; by it I mean little more than Karl Barth, who much earlier in this century said that

> The church is witness of the fact that the Son of man came to seek and to save the lost. And this implies that—casting all false impartiality aside—the Church must concentrate first on the lower and lowest levels of human society. The poor, the socially and economically weak and threatened, will always be the object of its primary and particular concern. . . .[3]

Barth's firm commitment to this theme is indicated in his willingness to draw as a correlate the conclusion: "We do not really know Jesus (the Jesus of the New Testament) if we do not know him as this poor man, as this (if we may risk the dangerous word) partisan of the poor. . . ."[4] It is in this sense that we may explore the significance of a "preferential option for the poor" in Wesley and the Methodist traditions without the fear of anachronism or of forcing our own modern categories on history.

The Wesleyan "Preferential Option for the Poor"

I have presented my interpretation of this theme in Wesley more fully in my November, 1990, presidential address to the Wesleyan Theological Society, the week of the publication of Theodore Jennings' book *Good News to the Poor: John Wesley's Evangelical Economics*,[5] with which I am generally in basic agreement. My fundamental reservation about that book is that, while we can probably agree with Jennings that "every aspect of Methodism was subjected to the criterion, how will this benefit the poor? " I am less convinced than Jennings that Wesley lifts this to the level of theological principle. His practice seems to make an option for the poor constitutive of the life of the church, but I am less clear how he would argue the theological grounding for this praxis.[6] It seems to me that one reason for the neglect of this theme in later generations is that Wesley did not ground his praxis sufficiently theologically to make the issue normative for those who would claim him as mentor in following centuries. No doubt we will be debating the various aspects of this question (Were the early Methodists really poor? Was this theme in Wesley an "accident" of the early years of Methodism? etc.) for some time to come. Meanwhile, however, let me summarize my own tentative and preliminary view of the matter.

First, anyone who has read at all in the *Journal* of Wesley will know that Wesley was systematic in his cultivation of the poor. He made it a regular practice from his Oxford student days to visit the sick, the poor, and those in prison, and he regularly insisted that his followers do likewise. He urged "a member of the society" in 1776 "frequently, nay, constantly to visit the poor, the widow, the sick, the fatherless, in their affliction."[7] Wesley's commitment to this practice is made clear in his sermon "On Visiting the Sick" based on the classic text of Matthew 25. In this sermon Wesley argued that the visiting of the poor is an absolute duty of the Christian without which one's "everlasting salvation" is endangered. Wesley built into the life of

Methodism collections for the poor and on occasion went publicly begging for the poor.

Second, Wesley's struggle with and final acceptance of field preaching must surely also be related to this theme. It is no accident that his first major experience with this practice was a sermon based on Luke 4:18-19, a key text for "liberationist" readings of Scripture or any advocacy of a "preferential option for the poor." After a brief experience preaching in Nicolas Street on April 1, 1739, Wesley initiated the practice on the next day (a Monday):

> At four in the afternoon, I submitted to be more vile, and pro-claimed in the highways the glad tidings of salvation, speaking from a little eminence in a ground adjoining to the city, to about three thousand people. The scripture on which I spoke was this, (is it possible any one should be ignorant, that it is fulfilled in every true minister of Christ?) "The Spirit of the Lord is upon me, because he hath anointed me to preach the Gospel to the poor. He hath sent me to heal the broken-hearted; to preach deliverance to the cap-tives, and recovery of sight to the blind: to set at liberty them that are bruised, to proclaim the acceptable year of the Lord."[8]

Third, it is also possible to argue that Wesley's message was peculiarly adapted to the poor—that for some fundamental reasons "the poor heard him gladly." Robert D. Hughes III grounds this directly in Wesley's theology—in his "Arminian evangelicalism" with its "twin pillars of universalism and insistence on the role of man's free will in salvation."[9] These principles meant that *all* (even the poor and "disreputable") could come and find acceptance in the Gospel and in the societies of Methodism. In *The Methodist Revolution* Bernard Semmel makes the same point through the doctrines of Christian Perfection and Assurance, "an experience more accessible to the humble and unsophisticated than to their better situated or better educated fellows."[10] Wesley's brand of Methodism affirmed the magisterial Reformation "pessimism of nature" but went on to profess an "optimism of grace" that offered the hope of change— both personally and socially. This is the revolutionary side of Meth-odism that offered hope to the poor.

Fourth, however we make the case, I think that it is clear that Wesley's theology and preaching tended toward a profound "gospel egalitarianism" that the poor found attractive. Wesley used the gos-pel radically to relativize a variety of factors that often sustain class structures and thus oppress the poor in various subtle and not so subtle ways: education, birth, social class, etc. As the Duchess of Buckingham wrote to the Countess of Huntingdon, significantly the patron of George Whitefield and the "Calvinistic" wing of the Methodist movement:

> I thank your ladyship for the information concerning the Methodist preachers. Their doctrines are most repulsive, and strongly tinctured with impertinence and disrespect towards their superiors, in perpetually endeavoring to level all ranks, and do away with all distinctions. It is monstrous to be told that you have a heart as sinful as the common wretches that crawl on the earth. This is highly offensive and insulting, and I cannot but wonder that your ladyship should relish any sentiment so much at variance with high rank and good breeding.[11]

Fifth, no doubt the poor were also attracted to Wesley because he did not blame them for their poverty. "So wickedly, devilishly false is that common objection, 'They are poor, only because they are idle.'"[12] Wesley's favoritism for the poor was also revealed negatively by his hostility toward the rich, as evidenced in many of his sermons that we tend to neglect because they fall outside the "standard sermons" that we more usually consult: "The Danger of Riches" (#87); "On Riches" (#108); "The Rich Man and Lazarus" (#112); "On the Danger of Increasing Riches" (#126). If anything, Wesley became more cranky on this issue as he grew older and more worried about the departure of Methodism from his principles. In this sense Wesley did not shirk, as do many modern advocates of a soft version of a "preferential option for the poor," from the "woes" against the rich that parallel the "beatitudes" that bless the poor (especially in Luke's version).

We could explore other aspects of Wesley's commitment to the poor: the role of his extensive publishing program in the education of the poor; his concern for health; Methodist structures for the relief of the poor; and so forth. But I must move on to the question of how Wesley grounded and defended his concern for the poor. I have hinted above that Wesley seems to have made visiting the sick and the poor a dimension of discipleship without which one's salvation is endangered. Very occasionally he appealed to the precedent of the life of Jesus and the Apostles.[13] Other times Wesley implies an egalitarianism based in the death of Jesus for all without distinction.[14] He also hints that the character of grace may be at stake: "Religion must not go from the greatest to the least, or the power would appear to be of men."[15] But as I have explored these passages, I do not think that I find a self-consciously theological articulation of the grounds for this "preferential option for the poor." In this lack of such a grounding, I believe that we see a major flaw in the Wesleyan articulation of this principle that contributed, along with other factors, to a profound ambiguity in the Wesleyan legacy on this question.

A Fundamental Ambiguity in the Wesleyan Legacy

Wesley himself was aware of the difficulty of sustaining the Methodist "preferential option for the poor" over time. Viewed from the perspective of this essay, his often-quoted words of warning to the Methodists gain a new poignancy:

> Does it not seem (and yet this cannot be) that Christianity, true Scriptural Christianity, has a tendency, in process of time, to undermine and destroy itself? For wherever true Christianity spreads, it must cause diligence and frugality, which, in the natural course of things, must beget riches! and riches naturally beget pride, love of this world and every temper that is destructive of Christianity.[16]

Wesley pointed in this and other similar comments to the dynamic that "church growth" specialists call the "social uplift" effect of Christian movements that find new vitality in a turn toward the poor but are soon drawn away from the life of the poor by new disciplines and other factors that pull them toward the middle classes, a tendency that we may celebrate or regret depending on other commitments.

I often wonder how to interpret the epigraph from Wesley with which I began this paper. Why is it that the "greatest miracle of all" is that the "poor have the Gospel preached to them"? Could it be that sociological and cultural forces are so pitted against such a result that when it occurs it can only be a "miracle of grace"? And if a "preferential option for the poor" is a central theme of the Gospel and the biblical witness, should we move to think of those powers that pull us away from this task as the epitome of sin—as a form of "original sin" in which our desire for respectability and acceptance puts us in fundamental opposition to this basic theme?

Full analysis of this dynamic, this war within the soul of Methodism in which the movement is drawn both toward the poor and away from the poor, is beyond the purposes of this essay, but it would seem to have several layers. There is an obvious sociological dynamic to which Wesley seems to be pointing in the quotation above. Such movements, especially those with a rigorous and highly disciplined ethical standard and the expectation of a radically transformed life under grace, bring a new discipline and focus to life that provides a form of upward social mobility that draws the movement more and more into the bourgeois middle classes and forms of church life, a process that I have frequently called *embourgeoisement*.[17] But there is also a profound psychological dimension—a powerful urge to overcome the alienation from the culture caused by the marginalization of poverty and belonging to religious movements that are not carriers of central cultural values. This urge expresses itself most powerfully in the second and third generations among those who are reared from childhood within the life of such new movements. There is the powerful urge to "belong," to find a role at the center of the culture, and especially to move beyond the disreputable aspects of a "deprived background." The "liberationist" analysis has helped us to understand the extent to which oppression trains the oppressed to envy their oppressors and pattern their own lives after patterns of their own oppression.

As in most similar movements, there was in Wesley's legacy a profound ambiguity of countervailing forces. On the one hand, there was the model of Wesley in turning toward the poor—in field preaching; in planting churches among the lower middle classes, the working classes, and the poor; and so on. And, on the other hand, there were the profound sociological and psychological forces that pulled Methodism away from the poor—and back toward the more "respectable" established church and toward the center of the culture. These countervailing forces created a highly unstable Methodist mix that would shape the successive history of the Methodist traditions—and indeed the wider Christian world, since it is probably impossible to understand the life of Protestantism apart from Methodism. At times certain wings of Methodism would reassert, and on occasion even radicalize, the Wesleyan "preferential option for the poor." At other times certain other wings of Methodism, or the same wings in other times, would play out the other trajectory and move away from the poor. This fundamental ambiguity lies at the very heart of those currents that claim Wesley as a founder; Methodist history since Wesley must be interpreted in terms of this struggle in the very soul of our movements.

But to this constitutional instability of Methodism with regard to its relationship to the poor we must add a further dimension of theological and ecclesiastical instability in the life of Methodism. We see this conflict most sharply in the ongoing conflict between what I will somewhat reluctantly call the "high church" and the "low church" interpretations of Wesley and the Methodist experience. Perhaps the clearest illustration of what I mean here is to be found in the book *The Believers' Church: The History and Character of Radical Protestantism* by Donald F. Durnbaugh.[18] Though quite conscious of the difficulty of putting Methodism squarely in the category indicated in the title of his book, Durnbaugh does treat Methodism and provides an interesting analysis focused in the diagram on the following page.

This diagram is an effort to place the major Christian traditions in relationship to each other in a more sophisticated version of Troeltsch's sect/church typology. What is important for our purposes is that Durnbaugh puts the Methodists right in the center with arrows indicating that they may move in either a more radical or a more traditional direction depending on the historical circumstances and other factors in the life of Methodism in a given time. In Durnbaugh's words, "the middle ground is occupied by movements which are inherently unstable."[19] In this sense Methodism is constitutionally unstable, perhaps the most constitutionally unstable of all Christian movements, at least according to Durnbaugh.

I have analyzed further this theological "constitutional instability" of Wesleyanism in my book *Theological Roots of Pentecostalism*.[20] In one sense, I am suggesting little more than Albert Outler when he described Methodism as an "ecumenical bridge" tradition with points of contact with the whole range of Christian traditions, or when Colin Williams suggests that Wesley kept in balance Catholic, Magisterial Protestant, and Radical Protestant elements in a sort of "catholic" synthesis.[21] But the fundamental question is whether these diverse tendencies are held together in a principled matter in Methodism or whether in Wesley's time they were held together merely in the particularity of his own mind and personality, only to fragment in the age after Wesley. There is evidence on both sides of this question, and there is reason to celebrate the genius of Wesley and the Methodist tradition in attempting to hold these diverse elements together. But the point for us here is that Methodism is a highly complex and unstable synthesis in which the constituent parts are

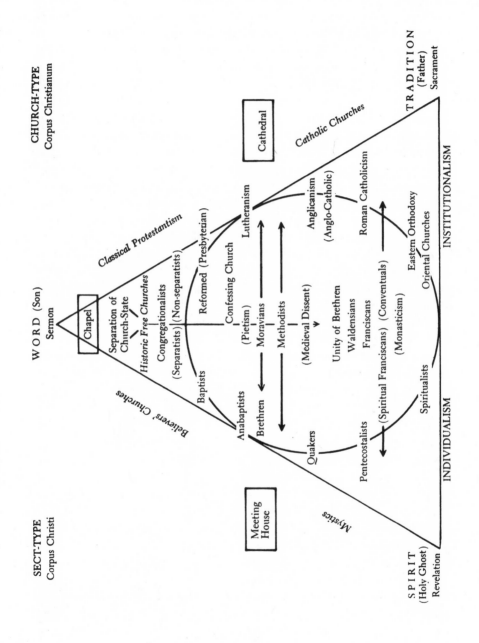

likely to fly apart into fragments, each of which has a genuine rootage in Wesley but yet has difficulty recognizing the Wesleyan dimension in the other. Thus the campmeeting tradition rooted in a sense in Wesley's field preaching has difficulty recognizing Wesley in the more traditional forms of church life rooted more in Wesley's high-churchmanship, and vice versa.

Our present interests here are also more in the correlation of these two "instabilities," the theological and the sociological. Without trying to enforce a rigorous conformity to our paradigm and recognizing some counter evidence, I think it is nonetheless clear that there is a correlation between the countervailing movement toward the poor and away from them with the theological fragmentation of Methodism. It is the revivalist and campmeeting side of the Methodism that has most faithfully preserved the Wesleyan "preferential option for the poor," cultivated the Wesleyan use of the laity, extended the Wesleyan openness to the ministry of women, and in general preserved a "low-church" reading of Wesley. It is the more classical and traditional side of Methodism that has brought Methodism more into the cultural center, has pushed toward the professionalism of the ministry, has more faithfully preserved the complexity of Wesleyan thought with its classical and traditional tendencies, and in general been the carrier of a more "high-church" reading of Methodism.

An Alternative Historiography?

In a modest sense we might find here a new "historiography" of the Methodist experience, one that would place this "war" of countervailing forces at the center of our focus to find a perspective that would revise many of our ways of reading that tradition. Such a reading might provide insight not only into the fate of our theme, the "preferential option for the poor," among Methodists, but also to wider dynamics in the life of Methodism.

I have come to many of these insights pursuing the history of the emergence of the ministry of women in the church in general, but especially in the Methodist traditions. This study has forced me radically to revise many inherited patterns of thought, especially those that insist on dividing the world, especially the church world, into the categories of "liberal" and "conservative," a lens for viewing the world that seems almost unavoidable in the twentieth century and, perhaps especially in North America, in the wake of the conflicts of the fundamentalist/modernist controversy. If we spread the Methodist traditions along such a spectrum, it is surprisingly the so-called "conservative" traditions that have been more open to the ministry of women while the "progressive" traditions have more often suppressed such a disreputable practice in their efforts to show that they "belong" in the center, at least until that point in the twentieth century when the basic tenets of feminism became generally accepted culturally and thus one of the elements that one needed to affirm to be accepted in the broader culture.

To understand such dynamics we need to use more subtle and complex paradigms of thinking to overcome the superficiality of the conservative/liberal spectrum. We should find other patterns of thought, perhaps in the diagram of Durnbaugh above, or in a dynamic of (perhaps alternating) centrifugal/centripetal movements away from and back toward the cultural center. Such ways of speaking would allow us more accurately to describe some of those movements within Methodism that we often label "conservative" as actually "radicalizations" of the Methodist impulse, sometimes in ways that go far beyond Wesley. The "campmeeting" traditions of Methodism, for example, are only in a few very specialized ways "conservative;" they more often are "radicalizations" of one side of Wesley that pull the Methodist tradition even further away from bourgeois church life, traditional views of the sacraments, classical theologies, "conservative" or "traditional" views of the ministry, and so on.

Such reorientations in my thinking have aided me in my attempts to offer more adequate interpretations of what constitutes the "evangelical" experience, the analysis of which consumes so much energy in our own time. "Liberal" is not a good antonym for "evangelical." This use of the words implies that "evangelicals" occupy the "center" of the Christian tradition now deserted by "liberals" who have left this space under the pressure of "modernity." This rather static analysis cannot explain the change in such movements over time, nor the rapid oscillation back and forth by such movements. Because the "conservative/liberal" paradigm helps us to analyze hardly anything historically, we should move beyond it in the analysis of Methodism itself.

With this preliminary call for new paradigms of analysis and perhaps even of a new "historiography" of Methodism, let us turn then to some historical illustrations of the playing out in history of this "constitutional" instability of the Wesleyan legacy.

The Challenge of Race Posed by the African American Methodists

Our first historical illustration is North American not only because of chronology but because it was in that context that Methodism most profoundly struggled with the question of race in the last decades of the eighteenth century. It may be part of the "epistemological advantage of the oppressed" that it was the African Americans who perhaps most clearly discerned this ambivalence of the Methodist tradition in its movement toward and away from the poor, and in many ways anticipated the historiographical perspective that I have suggested above.

It was no accident in the late eighteenth and early nineteenth centuries that African Americans moved toward the Methodist and Baptist traditions—or that the African American churches tend still today to be largely Methodist and Baptist, with the addition of the more recently formed Pentecostal tradition. Richard Allen, for example, was faithful to the Methodist tradition and thankful for its mediation of the gospel:

> The Methodists were the first people that brought glad tidings to the colored people. I feel thankful that I ever heard a Methodist preach. We are beholden to the Methodists, under God, for the light of the Gospel we enjoy; for all other denominations preached so high-flown that we were not able to comprehend their doctrine. Sure I am that reading sermons will never prove so beneficial to the colored people as spiritual or extempore preaching. I am well convinced that the Methodist has proved beneficial to thousands and ten times thousands. It is to be awfully feared that the simplicity of the Gospel that was among them fifty years ago, and that they conform more to the world and the fashions thereof, they would fare very little better than the people of the world. The discipline is altered considerably from what it was. We would ask for the good old way, and desire to walk therein.[22]

By the "semi-centenary" of the African Methodist Episcopal Church (1866) Bishop Daniel A. Payne, who became the first formal historian of the movement, had worked out an historiographical framework for the understanding of the impact of Methodism that almost exactly fits what we have developed above. At this point, however, we are less interested in his accuracy than his perspective, his experience of Methodism from the underside, so to speak. His jubilee interpretation struggled with the notion articulated by a Black clergyman at a recent General Assembly of the New School Presbyterians that "Methodism degrades the Negro." Payne's great concern in his book is to trace the "ennobling" and "uplifting" impact of Methodism on all that it touches. He takes it as a fundamental principle of history

> that some men are apparently modest and good, while they are poor, but as soon as they become rich, their consequent influence begets pride and contempt, which lead them to acts of oppression against the weak, the poor and the defenseless.[23]

In Payne's view the Wesleys were raised up in response to the Church of England having fallen prey to such forces. The task for the Wesleys was "to convert the most vicious of the English peasantry," and to do so, "this apostolic band entered the public grounds, the alms-houses, the mines and the jails—expounding in simple speech the profound truths of Christianity. . . ." Interestingly, in Payne's view, they also "entered the mansions of the rich gentry and culti-vated nobility, subjecting many of them to the *Rule of Jesus.*" For Payne, Methodism is a double-edged sword, "a power exalting the lowly, humbling the powerful."[24] As successive African American interpreters have noticed, Payne's book at points reveals what seems at times to be an excessive reverence for education and something that might be called a naive doctrine of inevitable "progress." The ennobling impact of Methodism upon the "Anglo-Saxon" race is found in the production of literature, in the founding of schools and colleges, in the founding of Sunday-Schools, and finally in the sup-port of Christian missions—in ways in each case that were particu-larly adapted to the poor.

Payne goes on to develop similarly the impact of Methodism on the "Anglo-American" race in a second section of the book before turning to the impact of Methodism on the Negroes. Here he repeats the observation of Allen that Blacks were attracted to Methodism: "Among the early *converts to Christ*, by the agency of Methodist preachers, were many Negroes" who "naturally joined the Method-ist Episcopal Church."

> As long as this Church were in *number few*, and in *condition poor*, its *colored members were gladly received and kindly treated*, but as soon as

77

it began to increase in numbers and wealth, so it became elevated in social position—with this increasing prosperity, the enslaved and proscribed free Negro became contemptible in its eyes—this contempt culminated in such treatment of the colored members, as none but *men robbed of true manhood* could endure.[25]

This passage is followed by an extended quotation from the book of James about the honoring of the rich, a text that has always been a favorite of those advocating a "preferential option for the poor." In Payne's book the quotation ends with:

hath not God chosen the poor of this world rich in faith, and heirs of the Kingdom which he hath promised to them that love him? But ye have despised the poor. Do not rich men oppress you, and draw you before the judgment seats? Do they not blaspheme that worthy name by which you are called? If ye fulfil the royal law according to the Scripture, *thou shalt love thy neighbor as thyself*, ye do well. But if ye have respect to persons, ye commit sin, and are convinced of the law as transgressors.[26]

I find it difficult to follow the logic of Payne in this section. He introduces it with a summary of the biblical argument for the equality of races, that God "hath made of *one blood* all nations of men." Payne then proceeds to argue that because of this unity of the race "Methodism" cannot "degrade the Negro"—or else "Methodism would cease to be Methodism."[27] Apparently it is certain "Methodists" rather than "Methodism" in general that have oppressed the African because Payne goes on to show how the African Methodist Episcopal Church itself has moved on to support the "education" and other forms of "social uplift" for the African American that he has celebrated among the "Anglo-Saxons" and the "Anglo-Americans." We must assume then, at least in the view of Payne, that the line of "true Methodism" moves from the first generation of the Wesleys through the first generation of the American Methodism to the emergence of the African Methodist Episcopal Church. We are left to wonder about the fate of Methodism in the next generation.

African American interpreters of Payne have not been too kind to him. No doubt Payne's reading of history is on one level naive and over-simplified, especially in its apparent commitment to education as a panacea for the evils and sins of the human race. Some of Payne's Black critics suggest that his own classism was revealed when he later felt impelled to resist the influx of the ex-slave preachers who were not quite up to his own standards of "respectability." Even the

African American tradition in one sense experienced the limits of toleration to challenges to its own self-interest that qualified its own commitment to a "preferential option for the poor" that would reach beyond its own boundaries! But in this, it is no different than any of the traditions we will examine. We are not left with the freedom to dismiss entirely his historiography, for Payne clearly discerned this fundamental conflict at the heart of Methodism. And it is clear that race constituted one of the most fundamental challenges to Methodism, especially in North America, and that by and large Methodism failed the test. If the Wesleyan "preferential option for the poor" is an essential ingredient of Methodism or of the biblical gospel then, then Daniel Payne may be correct in his tracing of a line of "true Methodism" that finds it difficult to sustain itself over generations.

The Growing Fragmentation of Methodism: The Primitive Methodists

Race was not the only factor that led to the fragmentation of Methodism and the formation of various traditions of Methodism. The theological and ecclesiastical instability of Methodism also manifested itself on both sides of the Atlantic in the decades after Wesley's death. Some branches of Methodism played out the trajectory of the more radical side of Wesley while others drew back toward the more classical tradition and toward a more "respectable" style of church life. Methodism got caught up in the tensions produced by the spread of a democratic egalitarianism, which only exacerbated the inner struggle of Methodism between its radical push toward a "gospel egalitarianism" and the drawing back toward more traditional styles of church life and organization. On both sides of the Atlantic profound struggles emerged that led to splits over a variety of divisive issues: the extent to which democratic structures of government ought to prevail within the life of Methodism, the role of the laity in church governance, the even more radical question of the role of women in ministry, the nature of ministry and ordination in general, the value and necessity of an educated ministry, the nature of Methodist worship, the use of the prayer book and formal liturgy, the status of the sacraments in Methodist worship, congregational singing versus the use of musical instruments and the propriety of professional musicians, the structuring of the church in general, modes of financing church life, whether the "pew rental" system was an appropriate way of financing church life, the appropriateness of "field preaching," the accountability of independent evangelists to larger church structures, campmeetings and their role in the life of the church, revivalism in general as a reading of Wesley and the heart of the Methodist impulse, and so forth.

We could take any of a number of examples of the splits over such issues. I have chosen to look at the emergence of Primitive Methodism and its conflicts with the more dominant Wesleyan Methodism to illustrate the dynamics in this period. Any selection of a case study during this period has its pros and cons. Primitive Methodism was in part (though only in part) a product of the American influence of Lorenzo Dow and his importation of the "campmeeting" tradition from North America. This fact may confuse the matter, and divert our discussion into a debate about "revivalism," but it also illustrates the transatlantic character of most of the conflicts of this era. I have chosen this illustration primarily to move us back across the Atlantic again to the nation of Wesley, and to pick up the largest and most powerful of the divisions within British Methodism. We could approach the analysis of this division in a number of ways. Let me briefly suggest some dimensions.

On a superficial level we might be inclined to interpret the rise of Primitive Methodism primarily in terms of the conflicts between powerful personalities. There is something to be said for this perspective. Much ink has already been spilt in the analysis of the role of Jabez Bunting in the period after Wesley. Bunting dominated the development of the Wesleyan branch of Methodism so much that he became known as the "Methodist Pope." Though earlier in his life more committed to at least some forms of "revivalism" and an advocate of the nondenominational "Sunday Schools," Bunting moved eventually to resist the influence of revivalism and the camp meetings traditions, to bring the Sunday Schools and other educational efforts under denominational control, to push strongly for the value of theological education and an educated ministry, to defend a form of clerical authority against the claims of the laity, and in general to centralize authority against those like Hugh Bourne and William Clowes who in many ways represented a free spirit that resisted such moves and found themselves expelled by the Wesleyans. Bourne and Clowes moved to found the Primitive Methodists and in the polarization to emphasize the opposite side of these tensions, commitment to the ministry of the laity and their role in church governance, freedom to employ women in ministry, dedication to the structures of the camp meeting and the spirit of "revivalism" in general, and so forth.

John Kent, Reginald Ward, and others have analyzed these conflicts as a struggle between a "high church" and a "low church" Methodism.[28] At the time the polemics were often cast between "primitive" and "modern" Methodism. David Hempton summarizes the position of Ward, himself a product of "Primitive Methodism," as follows:

> Professor Ward's analysis of Methodism and revivalism has stood up well. . . . The crude informality of the of provincial revivalists challenged the respectable ecclesiastical ambitions of a Wesleyan elite based on wealth, connexions and education. This elite responded to revivalistic enthusiasm with the attitude that "what was needed was less revival and more denominational drill"; less expansion and more consolidation. Thus, Ranterism, which challenged Wesleyanism hard where it "teetered between form and formalism," encouraged the very thing it was reacting against—a more rigid denominationalism.[29]

This fundamental conflict was then played out in terms not only of style but also in more theological terms of visions of the church, the nature of ministry, forms of worship, and so forth.

But it is also clear that such issues, as is hinted at in the above quotation from Ward, had their roots in social class conflict. Again, one cannot absolutize such claims in the face of some contrary evidence, but most interpreters agree that the Primitives tended to find success in a level of society lower than that of the Wesleyans. This is the regular conclusion of observers both at the time and in the more recent scholarship, for example, Julia Stewart Werner, who comments:

> Where Wesleyan Methodism was deeply rooted and the Wesleyan itinerants both encouraged revivalism and permitted a greater than usual degree of lay involvement, Primitive Methodism prospered least. In circuits like Manchester and Bolton, however, whose Wesleyan and New Connexion preachers aligned themselves with the middle class and stifled lay initiative, disenchanted Methodists were eager to embrace the sectarian alternative of Ranterism.[30]

In summary, she says:

... the conversion tactics of the new sect, its fostering of lay enterprise, and the sense of community that characterized its societies fulfilled needs increasingly felt among the lower classes as they moved from a dependent and traditional pattern of life into the new ways of a rapidly evolving urban industrial nation. Primitive Methodism preempted a significant role that Wesleyan Methodism failed to play, and it undertook this mission precisely at the time when opportunities were greatest. In consequence, the Primitive Methodist Connexion ultimately became the preferred affiliation for many working class Methodists.[31]

In the Primitive Methodist literature that I have examined I have not found a full, self-conscious articulation of a "preferential option for the poor," but the kernel of the idea is clearly in the literature. John Petty's history describes the significance of the name as a call to "cultivate the simplicity and zeal, the faith and piety, by which the first Methodists were distinguished"—in part by "regular open-air preaching"—and to "preserve the life and fervour of apostolic Christianity; to maintain plain, pointed, and energetic preaching; to 'condescend to men of low estate.'..."[32] Or again, and more fully:

It has been mindful of the apostolical admonition, 'Mind not high things, but condescend to men of low estate.' It has usually left the wealthy and the polished classes of society to the care of the older denominations, while it has sought the enlightenment and elevation of the poor.[33]

Similar themes and perspectives are projected back on the early Christian church, where the apostles were " 'unlearned and ignorant,' or home-bred, possessing no extraordinary talents, and retaining much of their rough Galilean dialect and rusticity of manners."[34]

However one understands all of this, it is important to notice that Primitive Methodism played an important role in the emergence of the labor movement in Britain. A movement toward the poor often reshapes one's politics, even if, in some cases, it becomes a simple case of self-interest. This more radical branch of Methodism was a carrier of a more radical social tradition than the Wesleyan wing. As John Munsey Turner put it,

Primitive Methodism brought into the union of Methodists in 1932 men and women who combined a simple, almost Quakerly style, a deep concern for social justice brought out of the struggles for workers' rights in mining and in the agricultural struggles. Certainly a deep fissure had developed between religion and labour politics which has widened since. Primitive Methodism, even if seen as an interim faith, played a role in the painful birth of modern English socialism out of all proportion to is numerical size.[35]

The Free Methodists in North America

One of the sharpest and most profound articulations of the "preferential option for the poor" emerged in North America, in upstate New York, under the ministry of B. T. Roberts, the primary founder of the Free Methodist Church. For Roberts, the equivalent of Jabez Bunting was probably Bishop Matthew Simpson, who was a symbol of the new *embourgeoisement* of the Methodist Episcopal Church. Simpson was the editor of *The Cyclopedia of Methodism*, which surely must be understood, at least in part, as an effort to put Methodism more clearly on the ecclesiastical map. Simpson was a leader in advocating theological education and other efforts to lead American Methodism toward more traditional church life. Some of this was rooted in his travels in Europe and his respect for European culture and more traditional church buildings and music. He was in many ways a symbol of the *embourgeoisement* of Methodism in the generation before the Civil War in the United States. One can almost hear the collective sigh of relief of American Methodists at having finally arrived culturally when Bishop Simpson was asked to participate in the various funeral services of assassinated President Abraham Lincoln.

This new denomination of "Free Methodists" focused many of the issues that troubled Methodism on both sides of the Atlantic in the nineteenth century. The emerging church rejected the episcopacy and affirmed the equal representation of the laity in church governance. Roberts himself was deeply committed to the ministry of women, and was profoundly disturbed when his denomination failed to support him on this point toward the end of the century. The "free" in "Free Methodism" carried a great deal of freight. It signaled the new denomination's commitment to abolitionism, a concern to "free" the slaves (the one Free Methodist change in the "general rules" was to forbid the holding of slaves). It expressed a concern to articulate a version of the Wesleyan doctrine of "Christian Perfection" that enabled the Christian to live "free" from sin. It identified a style of worship that was congregational in style and "free" in spirit, as well as being "free" from musical instruments, paid professionals, and other innovations that turned worshippers into an audience of observers. It referred to the reaffirmation of a pattern of dress that would be "free from the outward ornaments of pride." There were other connotations to the word "free," including freedom from secret societies (a response to controversies over Free Masonry), but the primary meaning of "free" was a polemic against "pew rentals" and an assertion of commitment to a system of "free pews." This commitment to "free pews" was symbolic of a larger commitment to a church that would serve the poor and structure church life on their behalf.

This "free pews" theme permeates the writings of Roberts but his thinking on the question is epitomized in the lead article in the first issue of *The Earnest Christian* (January 1860), the heart of which was reprinted as the introduction to early *Disciplines* of the Church. This article is preceded by a description of the "object and scope" of the magazine, including that

> *The claims of the neglected poor*, the class to which Christ and the Apostles belonged, the class for whose special benefit the Gospel was designed, to all the ordinances of Christianity, will be advocated with all the candor and ability we can command.

The key article is entitled "free churches." B. T. Roberts argues that *"Free Churches are essential to reach the masses."* In making this case Roberts carefully balances both the universality of the gospel and its particular commitment to the poor. "The provisions of the gospel are for all...to civilized and savage, black and white, the ignorant and the learned, is freely offered the great salvation." But Roberts goes on to ask, *"for whose benefit are special efforts to be put forth?"* In answering this question Roberts makes an interesting appeal to Luke 7, where he links his answer directly to the messianic office of Jesus:

> Jesus settles this question. . . . When John sent to know who he was, Christ charged the messengers to return and show John the things which they had seen and heard. "The blind receive their sight, and the lame walk, the lepers are cleansed, and the deaf hear, the dead are raised up," and if all this would be insufficient to satisfy John of the validity of his claims, he adds, "AND THE POOR HAVE THE GOSPEL PREACHED TO THEM." This was the crowning proof that He was the One that should come. It does not appear that after this John ever had any doubts of the Messiahship of Christ. He that cared for the poor must be from God.

Roberts goes on to make this theme decisive for the church and the disciples of Jesus: "In this respect the Church must follow in the footsteps of Jesus. She must see to it, that the gospel is preached to the poor." This fact is grounded in the plan of God, who "hath chosen the foolish things of the world to confound the wise." But Roberts takes another step and moves on to make this theme defining of the nature of the church:

> There are hot controversies about the true Church. What constitutes it, what is essential to it, what vitiates it? These may be important questions, but there are more important ones. It may be that there cannot be a Church without a bishop, or that there can. There can be none without a gospel, and a gospel for the poor. Does a church preach the gospel to the poor—preach it effectively? Does it convert and sanctify the people? Are its preaching, its forms, its doctrines, adapted *specially* to these results? If not, we need not take the trouble of asking any more questions about it. It has missed the main matter. It does not do what Jesus did, what the Apostles did.[36]

This strikes me as a very remarkable theology and a very radical position. B. T. Roberts seems to be arguing that a "preferential option for the poor" is *defining* of the true church, that it belongs to its *esse* rather than to its *bene esse*. As such Roberts has more than any other in the Wesleyan tradition (at least that I have read) clearly articulated the Wesleyan "preferential option for the poor," grounding it theologically in the messianic office of Jesus and making it defining of the church, thus raising it to the level of the *status confessionis* of more confessional traditions.

It is worth noting also the way in which the "pew rental" theme and its correlate "preferential option for the poor" was the organizing principle of Roberts' theology and church practice. The early Free Methodist commitment to "plain dress" was *not* just a form of legalism, but was firmly grounded in a larger missional vision that said that all should dress to make the poor feel comfortable in their midst. Consistent Free Methodists "dress *down*" to go to church! Similarly, their commitment to "prohibition" and the Prohibition Party (for many years the Prohibition Party candidate for President in the United States was a Free Methodist) was not so much a campaign against alcohol as an issue of *personal* vice as such but rose out of a conviction of Free Methodists that alcohol oppressed the poor. Prohibition was a "social vision" that worked for a new society through the political process—and occasionally outside it, as in the ax wielding of Carrie Nation who was also associated with the Free Methodists. This commitment to the poor led to a range of political activity that one might not expect: a radical critique of capitalism, including an occasional tendency to favor a sort of "Christian socialism"; critiques of monopolies and emerging economic structures like the stock market; advocacy of the poor farmers, including forms of political activism on their behalf, and so on. And, at least in theory, there was a push to move beyond a patronizing view of the poor to a real vision of solidarity. As Roberts put it,

> A Christian goes among the poor—not with the condescending air of a patron—but with the feeling of a brother. . . . In the Christian congregation the rich and poor meet together on terms of equality, and no preference is given to a man on account of his riches, or his gay and costly apparel.[37]

It is not clear that Free Methodism has sustained this commitment any better than mainstream Methodism, but it has managed to produce some important advocates of a "preferential option for the poor." Free Methodism may also demonstrate that even a profound theological grounding of the principle may not serve to sustain the theme in the face of the forces that would erode it. Nonetheless it remains true that B. T. Roberts of the Free Methodist tradition was, at least historically, one of the clearest of the Methodist articulators of a "preferential option for the poor."

The Salvation Army as a Radicalization of Methodism

Many of us generally do not naturally consider the Salvation Army a branch of the Methodist tradition, but I think that it is clear that we should. Both William Booth and his wife Catherine had roots in the Reform traditions of Methodism, and William served New Connexion churches before his break. One famous picture in the Salvation Army literature shows William Booth waving to his Catherine in the gallery of a Methodist church. Booth was calling his wife to meet him at the door in a symbolic departure in impatience with church bureaucracy in meeting the needs of the poor. This symbolic shaking of Methodist dust off his feet led William Booth out of the Methodist tradition in a formal sense, but the movement continued to reveal the influence of especially the Holiness tradition of theology, perpetuated still today in the "holiness meetings" and doctrines of the Army, particularly perhaps in the United States.

This is no accident; the Army reflects again the transatlantic character of many of these movements in that William Booth was converted under the preaching of James Caughey, the American Methodist evangelist with revivalist and holiness leanings, and in that Catherine felt called to ministry and preaching during the "four years in the old world" of Phoebe Palmer, often considered the founder of the holiness movement. This influence of Phoebe Palmer probably led Catherine Booth to push William on the question of the ministry of women, a pressure that made the Army one of the most consistently feminist religious organizations in the nineteenth century.

The Army was more the praxeological incarnation of the Wesleyan "preferential option for the poor" than a theological articulation of the principle. By such measures as the adoption of the military style of dress and organization it managed to freeze its commitment to the poor into a "permanent sect" that gives us some continuing reflection of what many Holiness churches were in earlier years. Early Army literature is filled with polemic against the "respectable churches" and the claim to be the true followers of Christ, "who though he was rich, yet for our sakes became poor, that we, through his poverty, might become rich, and who had left us an example that we should follow in his steps."[38] Similar rhetoric appears throughout the Army literature, though not, so far as I have seen, with the same regular and systematic development of a "preferential option for the poor" as I have suggested appears, for example, among the Free Methodists.

There exist many parallels in the Army to the radical side of Methodist preaching. Booth remarks in his book *In Darkest England and the Way Out* that

> The Scheme of Social Salvation is not worth discussing which is not as wide as the Scheme of Eternal Salvation set forth in the Gospel. The Glad Tidings must be to every creature, not merely to an elect few who are to be saved. . . . It is now time to fling down the false idol, and proclaim a Temporal Salvation as full, free and universal, and with no other limitations than the "Whosoever will," of the Gospel.[39]

Here one finds many of the Wesleyan themes of a personal "gospel egalitarianism" overflowing into a social vision for the poor, though perhaps not with the same theological sophistication but with the same anti-Calvinistic polemic.

One also finds many of the same issues as the Salvation Army struggled with its status over against the churches. Was it to be like Wesley's Methodist movement before the separation, a movement of renewal and revitalization that met outside the "church hours" and so declined to become a church? Is this how, for example, we are to understand the Army tendency to avoid the use of the sacraments? Or was there a theological issue at stake, as David Rightmire argues, that the Army was a radicalization of the holiness movement away from traditional church life and a parallel radicalization of the holiness theological tendency to subordinate ecclesiology to pneumatology and thus reconceive the whole logic of Christian Faith?[40] Such is but a recasting of the issues that Methodism struggled with after Wesley's death.

From a modern view point we often see the Army as a traditional and sentimental view of charity, typified by the food-basket at Christmas. We forget what a threat the Army posed to the dominant culture by its "turn to the poor." In one twelve-month period around 1880, 669 Salvationists were reported "knocked down, kicked, or brutally assaulted," 56 Army buildings were stormed, and 86 Salvationists imprisoned. We forget what a threat it was to conventional morality to have William Booth argue that prostitution was not caused by lack of virtue but was the product of such social forces as low wages that could not support young women flocking to London or to reject the double standard of sexual morality on profoundly feminist grounds. We forget that the mere movement toward the poor to identify with the poor is often so profound a move that it threatens the whole culture and appears to be "subversive." W. T. Stead in a biography described Catherine Booth as a "socialist and something more" because she was "in complete revolt against the existing order."[41] And many of our modern day forms of social ministry have not advanced far beyond the scheme of "social salvation" of Booth with its credit unions, day care centers, shelters for the homeless and abused, legal assistance, and so forth, not to mention the various campaigns of political advocacy in which the Army engaged.

The Church of the Nazarene:
A "Preferential Option for the Poor"

The Church of the Nazarene was the major denominational product of the "holiness revival" in the United States. This revival had many sources, from the Finneyite revivalism that emerged in the increasing "Arminianizing" of New England Theology after Jonathan Edwards, through the cultural optimism of the age that was ready to receive Methodist perfectionist egalitarianism as a support for the emerging "democratic" vision in the new nation, to the Tuesday Meetings for the Promotion of Holiness in which Methodist lay-woman Phoebe Palmer led many Methodists and others into a form of the Methodist experience of "entire sanctification." The American Holiness Movement emerged out of the amalgamation of such currents, gathered force during the century, found expression in the National Campmeeting Association for the Promotion of Holiness (which has evolved into the present-day Christian Holiness Association), went through a period of fragmentation at the end of the century into local holiness associations and eventually into an agglutinative process that began to produce at the turn of the century a variety of new holiness denominations claiming fidelity to a sort of "campmeeting" version of the Wesleyan tradition.

There is a strong tendency to describe this movement (both within and without its boundaries) as a "conservative" or "evangelical" version of the Methodist tradition. I am more and more convinced that this is a superficial reading of the situation along the lines described above in our historiographical discussion. This movement is better described as a reaction to the nineteenth-century *embourgeoisement* of Methodism in North America. It is more a radicalization of the Wesleyan tradition than a "conservative" version of it, though it often identifies itself as a reaction to a perceived "liberalization" of the Methodist tradition. There is no doubt some element of truth to that perception, but I find issues of class conflict more explanatory of many phenomena than the conservative/liberal paradigm.

However one sorts out such questions, it is clear that most wings of the Holiness Movement continued some commitment to a "preferential option for the poor" with varying degrees of clarity and radicality. Charles G. Finney, the Presbyterian/Congregationalist evangelist who was so influenced by Methodism that his theology was called "Oberlin Perfectionism" and became a major source of Holiness thinking, was so committed to "free pews" that his followers founded a separate Presbytery committed to the principle. Even Phoebe Palmer, whose "parlor holiness" so shunned controversy over political issues like slavery that Free Methodist B. T. Roberts disassociated himself from her in spite of having felt her influence spiritually, was known for her involvement in the "Old Brewery," an early antecedent of the "rescue mission" and "settlement house" movements. It was explicitly acknowledged in the emerging National Campmeeting Association that a major motive was to cultivate the masses. The campmeeting was the vehicle designed for this purpose. The close affinity of the Holiness Movement with the Salvation Army (today a member of the Christian Holiness Association) is to be explained not only in terms of the shared commitment to the "holiness" version of Wesleyan theology but also in a shared polemic against high steeple churches that neglected the poor and the masses. Similar dynamics were present in the founding of the Pilgrim Holiness Church and Holiness movements that emerged from other denominations (especially the Christian and Missionary Alliance under the influence of Presbyterian turned Holiness preacher A. B. Simpson); both churches boasted of their commitment to the poor and neglected, especially of the cities. In a sermon based on Luke 4:18-19, A. B. Simpson announced his departure from his east side Manhattan church to work among poor immigrants. But let us turn to the Church of the Nazarene to indicate a particular focusing of this theme within the Holiness Movement.[42]

Phineas Bresee was a successful Methodist pastor who precipitated a crisis in California Methodism when he requested "location" to work with a rescue mission in the face of the concern of Methodist Episcopal Church leadership who wished him to continue founding and leading successful and substantial churches that contributed more to the advance of Methodism and its financial success. It was this issue more than "theology" or "conservativism" as such that precipitated the crisis that led to the founding of a major new denomination in the Wesleyan tradition. The very name of the Church of the Nazarene was chosen to signal a "preferential option for the poor"; it was meant to express the commitment of the church to the mission of the "lowly Jesus of Nazareth." The first stationery of the Church quoted Jesus, "Inasmuch as you have done it unto the least of these my brethren, ye have done it unto me." And the preface to the first Articles of Faith and General Rules of the new church in 1895 clearly alluded to work among the poor.[43] Bresee was quite explicit about these commitments:

> The first miracle after the baptism of the Holy Ghost was wrought upon a beggar. It means that the first service of a Holy Ghost baptized church is to the poor; that its ministry is to those that are lowest down; that its gifts are for those that need them the most. As the Spirit was upon Jesus to preach the gospel to the poor, so His Spirit is upon his servants for the same purpose.[44]

Bresee developed from this position a polemic against elaborate and expensive church buildings and other features of the Holiness "preferential option for the poor." But such sentiments were not Bresee's alone. They pervaded the life of the early church of the Nazarene. One paper started in Texas in 1906 was called *Highways and Hedges* and boldly proclaimed that "the respectable have had this call and rushed madly on after the things of this world" and claimed that "steeple-house church people are busy chasing dollars." This paper vowed to "open up a chain of missions in all of our large cities where real mission and slum work is pushed; and the poor and destitute looked after."[45]

Again, of course, it was very difficult to sustain these early commitments. Like the Free Methodists, the Nazarenes, again with some significant exceptions, have found ways to avoid and suppress this theme in their lives and churches. Certain wings of the church, like the organization of philanthropic agencies and some forms of urban ministry, still appeal to this history and rhetoric, but it is difficult to avoid the impression that this theme is no longer vitally alive in the church.

Latin American Pentecostalism Viewed in the Same Line

Where in the twentieth century is this centrifugal motion of a "Wesleyan preferential option for the poor" being played out? There might be several answers to this question. The *embourgeoisement* of the various holiness churches is producing its own powerful but little noticed reaction in a variety of places. One might also point to various social movements over the last century or so that have revitalized in new modes the Wesleyan "preferential option for the poor," but I am convinced that the place where the original dynamic of Methodism is being played out most clearly is in the rise of

Pentecostalism in our century. We are not accustomed to thinking in these categories, but I am again convinced that we must. We do not understand the full range of Methodist experience, or Methodism itself, in a sense, without attending to this phenomenon. In many ways Pentecostalism is the radicalization of the holiness impulse within the Methodist traditions, or perhaps more recently a reaction to the *embourgeoisement* of the holiness churches. The historical linkages between Methodism and Pentecostalism have been traced by H. Vinson Synan[46] and I have extended this argument on the theological level in my *Theological Roots of Pentecostalism.*[47]

The way in which this Methodist dynamic is being played out in our time is perhaps best seen in the South American country of Chile, where Pentecostalism is most firmly rooted in the Methodist tradition and is threatening to become the dominant religious force in the country to the point of challenging the Roman Catholic Church. Chilean Methodism has its roots in the early visits of William Taylor, the maverick missionary Bishop of American Methodism, who planted a fiercely independent form of Methodism around the world (Africa, Asia, South America, especially—after years of street preaching in the California "gold rush" at mid-century). The Methodism that Taylor planted was very close to the Holiness Movement that gave him much support and named Taylor University after him, and the "self-supporting" missions that Taylor founded were also unique and largely outside the control of "official" Methodist mission boards. Taylor's plan raised the laity to new roles, placed the missionaries and nationals on a more equal footing financially, encouraged structures of "self-support" that provided for a dimension of independence, and was so demanding that it appealed only to the "less cultured revivalist fringe of the Methodist church in the United States."[48] This naturally gave the Methodism of Chile a "holiness" tinge and laid the foundation for the emergence of Pentecostalism in this context.

The early twentieth century brought new Methodist missionaries to Chile more in the tradition of the modern rejection of revivalism. According to John Kessler this precipitated a conflict between North American missionaries bringing a more middle class and modern orientation into a context in which the more traditional revivalism was more effective where Methodism was still located primarily among the working classes. The first decade of this century led to a number of conflicts that included the emergence of Pentecostalism under the ministry of a North American, Willis C. Hoover, pastor of a large Methodist Church in Valparaiso. Hoover was, however, so indigenized and acculturated that he was accepted as a "national," and to this day it is difficult to get Chilean Pentecostals to admit that the movement is in any way dependent on the North American scene and not totally an indigenous movement. At any rate, Chilean Pentecostalism arose rather spontaneously among Methodists at the end of the first decade of this century and from those beginnings has grown to about fifteen percent of the population, enough to compete with the number of "practicing Catholics," to use that unhappy term. Missionaries from classical Pentecostal denominations did not begin to have major impact until mid-century.

The Methodist influence is still predominant in the names of denominations, in the preservation of infant baptism, episcopal church government, doctrine, and hymns. Chilean Pentecostals often see their most characteristic practice to be "street preaching" which they understand to be in the "apostolic" line of the "field preaching" practiced by John Wesley (generally ignorant of William Taylor as a significant carrier of the practice). My examination of the rather limited literature that I have available to me on Chilean Pentecostalism does not reveal any self-conscious articulation of a "Wesleyan preferential option for the poor," but there can be little doubt that in practice there was the equivalent. Studies of Chilean Pentecostalism tend to see the growth of the movement as a result of its turn to the flood of poor workers from the country to the city. And in this and other features, John Kessler judges that "Hoover maintained the essence of the Wesleyan tradition more faithfully than the Methodist missionaries who opposed him, and this has come to be recognized increasingly by the Methodists themselves."[49] In this context we need also to think of the recent book by David Martin, now an Anglican but with Methodist roots. In *Tongues of Fire: The Explosion of Protestantism in Latin America*, Martin argues that we must see the rise of Pentecostalism in Latin America as the third great wave of the Methodist impulse that flowered in Great Britain in the eighteenth century, in North America in the nineteenth century, and now in Latin America in the twentieth century. Martin uses the categories of his Methodist background to provide one of the most powerful and useful interpretations of Pentecostalism to date.[50]

Such suggestions bring pause to our usual interpretations of

Pentecostalism, but they suggest that to predict the future of Latin American Pentecostalism in the next century, we need to look at North American Methodism in this century. What now appears as a somewhat otherworldly movement of the disenfranchised may prove to have a powerful social impact. There are already some signs of unexpected developments.[51] It is from the Chilean Pentecostals that the majority of Pentecostal members of the Work Council of Churches have come, and the indigenous character of the Chilean Pentecostal churches may give them freedom to move in new directions apart from the influence of North America. On a recent visit to Chile I was privileged to visit a congregation of the "Mision Wesleyana Nacional" whose founder had served on the *junta* of the Socialist Party of Chile in part out of his formation in the southern mining district of Chile.[52] Shades of early Methodism, the Primitive Methodists, and other brands of the Methodist tradition that have often broken into a form of social radicalism rooted in a "Wesleyan preferential option for the poor"!

Some Concluding Observations

I am aware of the limitations and modest results of this study, which has in many ways been narrowly focused on one strand of a Methodist "preferential option for the poor." I have not dealt with a more modern form of such a concern as would be expressed in the nineteenth-century move toward a more holistic social analysis as expressed in the social gospel, the "social principles" of the modern ecumenical movement, or more recently the questions raised by the theologies of liberation. This is not to deny their significance nor to suggest that there is not much to learn from them. Such currents have often had significant roots in the Methodist traditions. I would welcome such study but have felt that such was beyond the limits of my own essay. But, in this concluding section, I would like to suggest something of what I have intended here.

(1) I have suggested that there is buried in the Methodist tradition a very significant and profound history of a "Wesleyan preferential option for the poor" that deserves study and pondering. It does not answer all the questions that we have about this theme in the Methodist experience, but I believe that it speaks more profoundly to them than we might suppose. While not primarily political in the first sense, it has often given impulse to political currents and raised

significant political questions, both within the movements that it has generated and in the social radicalization that has come as persons have responded to a "preferential option for the poor" and shifted social location enough to gain a real sympathy for the poor.

(2) I have intended to unsettle our thinking by celebrating the "underside" of the Methodist experience, the side that most of us find somewhat disreputable and from which many of us are in various ways fleeing, and I have on occasion deliberately used provocative language to drive this point home. For a variety of reasons we scholars are all trained to read the Methodist tradition through the lens of the dominant and "higher" Methodist traditions, but we also need to reverse this lens and read the Methodist experience from the bottom up as well. Only by doing so will we ever really understand the internal dynamic of Methodism and the profound social influence that it has had.

(3) I have also tried to suggest that our readings of Methodist history might be informed by a "new historiography" more rooted in this "underside" of Methodist history, and that we may find here many clues not only about the social impact of Methodism but about the soul and fundamental intention of Methodism, issues that I am convinced remain unresolved in the life of our traditions.

(4) It should be clear that I have had an ecumenical intention in this essay. I have tried to put the "disreputable" traditions of Methodism at the table with the more traditional forms of Methodism in a way to open up a new dialogue about the nature of Methodism. I am convinced that we will understand Methodism fully only when such a dialogue takes place at a table of equals.

(5) It should also be clear that I have had a theological agenda as well. I have tried to suggest that Wesley bequeathed us a subtle synthesis, too subtle and complex (and perhaps idiosyncratic) to be kept together in one piece by the minds and cultural experiences that followed him. I am convinced that most of our traditions serve as carriers of only certain fragments of the tradition that disenfranchise and excommunicate each other as reflections of themes that cannot be genuinely "Wesleyan." We have hope of recovering the "historical Wesley" (and perhaps the spiritual inner dynamic of the Wesleyan tradition) only as we bring those pieces back together in the dynamic interaction that they had in Wesley.

(6) I have also sought to extend our view of what constitutes the broader Wesleyan tradition. For this reason I have included the

Salvation Army and Chilean Pentecostalism as illustrations of the Wesleyan tradition, and particularly of the power of its "preferential option for the poor." I am convinced that we will not fully understand the full range of the Methodist experience and power until we find a way to do this.

CHAPTER 5

Anointed to Preach:
Speaking of Sin in the Midst of Grace

REBECCA S. CHOPP

> The Spirit of the Lord is upon me,
> because he has anointed me
>   to preach good news to the poor.
> He has sent me to proclaim release
>   to the captives
> and recovery of sight to the blind,
> to set at liberty those who are oppressed,
> to proclaim the acceptable year of the Lord.
>   (Luke 4:18-19, RSV)

Introduction

God is a God of freedom and love. From creation to exodus to exile to Christ to church, the Scripture proclaims this reality over and over: God is a God of freedom and love. With the stirring words of Jesus' announcement of public ministry we have come to wrestle with the meaning of God as a living God of freedom and love in our day and age in the midst of our Wesleyan heritage.

Luke's words challenge and invite us to the mission of God and the church. To convey the import of Jesus, Luke selects the arena of history itself and so his Gospel begins with the genealogical narratives from the beginning of creation.[1] In Jesus, history is not escaped but reordered and transformed. Luke recaptures the Jubilee tradition that runs through the priestly and prophetic materials in the Hebrew Scriptures.[2] In the priestly tradition the Jubilee is the time in which society is radically reordered: the land gets redistributed, the oppressed are set free and relationships are organized through principles of justice. The prophet Isaiah picks up the Jubilee tradition and renders it eschatologically to portray God who will reorder all of history through justice and freedom. Then Luke has Jesus announce his mission as the fulfillment of the Jubilee: God's radical reordering of history.

As Jesus becomes the fulcrum point through which all of history is transformed, so the church is assigned the task of continuing the mission of transformation in the world. The church proclaims, mediates, and enacts God's mission of judgment and mercy. The church continues the solidarity of Jesus with the "others" of history: the poor, the oppressed, the marginalized, the downtrodden. If in Luke's gospel the "others" of history receive the power to speak and to determine their lives, then today the church exists amidst those who have received, in God's love and freedom, the power to proclaim the good news.[3] Luke challenges and invites us to begin where the church is in the ministry and mission of Jesus amongst the marginalized of the earth and from this place to work towards the transformation of history itself.

I shall develop, in a systematic fashion, a central theme of Wesleyan theology in relation to the option for the poor. A great amount of work exploring possible intersections between Wesleyan theology and liberation theology, particularly the option of the poor, has already occurred.[4] I want to work within the context of that conversation, but move to a somewhat different phase of the discussion in order to develop a Wesleyan theology operating from the option for the poor and oppressed in my own context in the United States. I understand my task as a systematic theologian in the Wesleyan tradition to fall under what Albert Outler has called Phase Three of Wesleyan Studies, the effort to apply Wesley to issues in our times and our future. More specifically, I hope to participate in this reformation of Wesleyan theology in our day which means, to follow Outler's thoughts on Wesley in Phase Three:

> . . . a *theology* less interested in the order of Christian *truth* (as in the school theologies generally) than in Christian *life*. Its specific focus is the order of salvation as an eventful process that stretches across the whole horizon of Christian existence. Its axial theme is *grace*, which makes it Christocentric and yet also preeminently pneumatological. For Wesley the Holy Spirit is the Lord and Giver of *Grace* as well as the Lord and Giver of Life. Thus, 'prevenience' is not a stage of grace but the crucial aspect of grace in all its manifestations.

It signifies the divine initiative in *all* spirituality, in all Christian experience. Wesley's theology is intensely evangelical but it looks also toward the ethical transformation of society.[5]

When, as a theologian in the Wesleyan tradition, I take seriously the axial theme of grace from the option of the poor in my own situation in the United States, I am led to think of what a discourse of sin might mean for the hegemonic culture in the United States. As occurs in any other theological paradigm, liberation theology finds that it must refashion and rework the doctrine of sin in relation to the contemporary situation, including the appropriation of current systems of thought and popular cultural images.

Yet to reconsider and reformulate the doctrine of sin for the dominant culture of the United States is not simply a requirement for the ongoing reformation of the Christian tradition but a rather desperate necessity for the hegemonic culture in the United States. Only a few books have been written on sin in the United States in the last thirty years; this absence allows many theologies of the center, despite their serious engagement with liberation theology, to continue being formulated through theological anthropologies and views of history with primary analogues to bourgeois existentialist or analytical philosophy.[6] I have a vision that one of the great gifts that the weaving together of liberation theology and Wesleyan theology can contribute to hegemonic cultures is a discourse of sin that names the reality of suffering and destruction, that criticizes unjust systems in need of correction, and that analyzes basic idolatrous forms of life in need of radical transformation. This discourse, which I will explore in this essay, is itself an act of grace, an act of divine initiative that speaks to a culture caught in the throes of idolatry of false gods of national, economic, racial, and sexual sovereignty, the concupiscence of consumerism, and the self-disintegration of isolated individualism.

The aim of my analysis will be to develop a discourse of sin that critically and analytically reveals the depravation and disorder of the hegemonic culture, that opens up the interlocking structures of injustice and oppression, and that identifies possible modes of transformation. If grace empowers us to see and speak of sin, grace also allows us, as Wesley so strongly maintained, not only to be justified but sanctified, not only to be emancipated from sin but transformed into new life. I will proceed with three specific steps to my argument:

first, I want to clarify some of my operating assumptions in terms of Christian prophetic movements in the United States, the alliance between contextual work and global solidarity, and the nature of systematic theology as I understand it. Second, I will develop a systematic proposal for a discourse of sin in relation to the hegemonic culture of the United States. Third, I want to conclude by suggesting how the discourse of sin correlates with expressions of sanctification in three areas: holy living, new forms of communities, and a poetics of hope in the North American context.

Prophetic Movements and Systematic Theology

By prophetic movements I mean the Christian movements that exist as an emergence of a distinct form of Christianity marked by the empowerment of the marginalized, the critique of hegemonic structures, practices and images, and the envisioning of new ways of life. For the past twenty-five years these movements have been expressed both inside and outside the institutionalized churches in the United States. Certainly many of the African American churches in the United States represent not only a recent reality of prophetic Christianity but also a long tradition of Christian response that cannot be solely identified with the dominant Christian participation in colonialism and, as Wesley would call it, the Gospel of Wealth. Feminist liberationist theology has important communal bases in the institutionalized church but also exists as a para-ecclesial form in women church communities. Feminist theology also has a long history in the United States with special roots in the Wesleyan movement, as Susie Stanley has argued in her essay "Empowered Foremothers: Wesleyan/Holiness Women Speak to Today's Christian Feminists."[7] As Stanley suggests, Wesleyan/Holiness women in the nineteenth century understood the authority of empowerment by the Holy Spirit in a fashion strikingly similar to the view of authority held by twentieth century feminists. As do twentieth century feminists, the women of the Wesleyan/Holiness movement identified their empowerment with an ethic for service aimed towards addressing social issues and alleviating social problems.

It may well be worth exploring what is the relation between these movements and the established institutional church. The adjectives "established" and "institutional" are important to note, for feminist liberation theologians have made very clear that *church* is identified first and foremost with the ecclesia that lives truly, that represents in sacramental fashion, the presence of God in the world.[8] Institutional churches, as Rosemary Radford Ruether has suggested, too often become occasions of sin, places where the poor are ignored, women belittled and humiliated, and the hegemonic practices receive religious reification.[9] Indeed, Wesleyan theologians working in the institutions of the established churches find themselves in a situation somewhat similar to Wesley's times. Not wanting to depart from the established churches, they nevertheless recognize the need to do more to address mission to the larger culture which the established churches fail to both challenge and serve.

Such prophetic movements commit themselves to be in global solidarity with the poor and the oppressed of the earth. I understand that to raise the question of the relationship between local contexts and global situations is itself to invite a rather complex discussion of current epistemological, aesthetic, and political terms. In the United States this is currently discussed under the terms of postmodernism and postcolonialism. I want only to observe, at this point, that cultural context and global solidarity are theologically related as well as structurally intertwined. As theologians we must pay attention both to the social reality that we live in a global environment and we must make this present in our theologies. But we also are making a theological claim about God, sin, and the transformation of all of creation. This is to suggest that not only do worldwide political structures bind us together, but as Christians we live and proclaim a worldwide solidarity in the name of the living God of love and freedom.

These two assumptions, the first concerning prophetic movements in the United States and the second concerning the relation of prophetic movements and global solidarity with the poor, leads to my third assumption about the nature of theology. As a feminist liberation theologian in the United States, I understand systematic theology to create spaces for empowerment, critique, and transformation through Christian community. As my reference to Outler's understanding of Wesleyan theology already suggests, in the Wesleyan tradition systematic theology focuses on grace-filled Christian living. My understanding of Wesley and the Wesleyan tradition in the context of my participation in feminist liberation movements means that the definition of theology shifts from mastering a closed system of doctrine to constructing open spaces for living. Indeed, one of the great contributions a Wesleyan feminist liberation theology has to make in North America is the expression of grace in the moments of empowerment, critique, and transformation in prophetic Christian movements.[10] In this way of doing theology doctrines become not the rules that control our behavior but the spaces, the ways of grace, that open us to mission. Thus we need to reconceptualize a Wesleyan systematic in ways that express how we understand life to be, and for us that is to take seriously the historical and structural constitutiveness of life, reformulating both the discourses of grace and sin in historical and structural terms.

In this manner I agree with José Míguez Bonino who has suggested that Wesley's theology must be rethought in two ways.[11] First we must rethink sanctification, the vision of the possible in the transforming power of grace, from the unity of creation and redemption. Second, we must rethink Wesley in light of the structural nature of social problems. This requires us to understand theology itself as transformative, as projecting transformation, and as structural, analyzing the depth structure of all of our life, including the interconnected realms of the political, the linguistic, and the subjective.

I want to introduce two terms to expand further how I understand systematic theology to be transformative. These two terms are often scoffed at, in a manner quite similar to the ongoing ridicule of both Wesleyan theology and feminist theology in ecumenical and academic circles. Perhaps we could even explore why the terms I choose to employ—pragmatism and rhetoric—are so often belittled along with Wesleyan and feminist theology. (My initial hunch as a starting point for such a conversation is that all have to do with contextual claims of transformation.) Pragmatism is often criticized as a form of functionalism and instrumentalism, but this is not accurate historically. Pragmatism, as a philosophical system, arose, according to Cornel West, out of the sufferings and destructions of the present age.[12] Pragmatism is characterized by a future orientation of thinking, as the critique of present and the imaginative projection of future possibilities. It is thus experimental, utilizing the logic of abduction which Charles Peirce defined as that which may be possible.[13] A pragmatist theology enacts, therefore, the desire for flourishing, the solidarity of our togetherness, and the anticipation of what is possible for each and for all.

But such transformative thinking must itself be historical, and thus we must retrieve and reconstruct the nature of systematic theology as rhetorical. Rhetoric is the attempt to persuade, to name, to be critical, to determine that which can be other.[14] In the philosophical tradition of the West, the art of rhetoric is tied to praxis for rhetoric arises out of the communal conditions of the present, and creates new possibilities for the future. I employ rhetoric because it is necessary to be attentive to the concrete conditions of life and to speak constructively in relation to the present situation and to use what is in our power, our words, to provide new transforming spaces for our cultures.

Theology, rethought through pragmatism and rhetoric, is itself transformative.[15] Its discursive function in the nature of the church's ongoing mission is to name sin and grace, to analyze the depravation and deprivation of our creaturely conditions, to imagine and construct sanctified ways of living. The hegemonic culture is, to use Luther's analogy, like a dying person who does not know he or she is ill and needs total care, including an adequate analysis of the disorder, treatment of the symptoms, healing, and a new way of living. A discourse of sin expresses the grace that gives us a detailed accounting and analysis of sin which itself leads to the envisionment of new ways of sanctified living.[16]

Structures of Sin

As Robert Chiles has noted, the distinctiveness of Wesley's theology is the way in which sin and grace are intertwined and enmeshed.[17] Grace allows us to be moved and to move against sin, grace not only restores us and redeems us but also transforms us. This precarious balance, as Chiles calls it, is noted nearly unanimously in the literature on Wesley.[18] What I want to explore is how this precarious balance has a necessary function in a feminist liberation theology in the United States.

We must begin, again, with a word of grace. Latin American liberation theology has been quite clear on the priority of God's grace, a claim often missed I fear by its readers in the United States. Gustavo Gutiérrez has insisted that the notion for the poor is first and foremost a claim about God's gratuitousness:

God's preferential option for the poor, the weak, the least members of society, runs throughout the Bible and cannot be understood apart from the absolute freedom and gratuitousness of God's love. . . . Universality and preference mark the proclamation of the kingdom. God addresses a message of life to every human being without exception, while at the same time God shows preference for the poor and the oppressed. . . . The gratuitous love of God requires that we establish an authentic justice for all, while giving privileged place to a concern for the unimportant members of society—that is for those whose rights are not recognized either in theory (by a set of laws) or in practice (in the way society conducts itself).[19]

It is this stress on the utter gratuitousness of God that is in liberation theology and in Wesleyan theology that sets the context for a powerful discourse on sin in the North American situation. An example will suffice to further my argument. Working with women across race and class lines in the United Sates one quickly discovers that the demons of patriarchy live within many women's internal feelings and thoughts, their souls and their words as well as in political, economic, and legal structures. What is required to break through the demonic powers of oppression and dehumanization internal to the woman, is the affirmation of the woman's self worth when all other messages—internal and external—tell her she's worthless, the lowest of the low, put on earth only to suffer. This ability to move a woman into her own self affirmation is, in my judgment, a current expression of grace.

It is the priority of this grace that allows the development of a discourse of sin aimed toward radical transformation in history. Within God's gratuitousness amongst the poor and the oppressed we name suffering, we criticize systems of injustice, and we analyze the depth structure of sin. Two sides of my argument should be noted. First of all, I am suggesting that a reformulation of the doctrine of sin is necessary in light of theological doctrine of sanctification in relation to the unity of creation and redemption and our current understandings of structural realities of life. Sin is, in my analysis, the depravation and deprivation of the flourishing of existence through concrete historical structures of politics, language and subjectivity. I want in my context to claim that sin is both depravation, the destruction of the basic conditions for life, and deprivation, the loss of the vision of flourishing.[20] Second, not only do I suggest a redefinition of sin, I want to opt for, at least in my context, three parts to each analysis of sin: the lamentation of suffering, critical theories of destructiveness, and an analytic of the depth structure of idolatry that runs through politics, language, and subjectivity.[21] A discourse of sin must describe reality, recollecting suffering and testifying to the disintegration and destruction of sin. A discourse of sin must lament the brokenness, the death, and the impoverishment of the human condition amidst present forms of oppression. But any discourse of sin must also try to uncover the conditions, interests and forms of false knowledge and power that creates such destruction through systems of injustice. A discourse of sin is in itself a resistance to injustice and the expression of the desire for human flourishing, for correcting all that is false, distorted, depraved. Yet the specificity of such a discourse also resides in its claims about the need for transformation and thus it must analyze the principles and practices of idolatry that run through all the forms of life. I recognize that I am calling for nothing short of a very large doctrine of sin in my context, yet for me this is the good news, the necessary news, the way to combine the universal love of God with the privileging of the oppressed.

The discourse of sin attempts, in the context of grace, to persuade persons of the actual situation in the world. It is a persuasive account that argues that suffering most adequately names common human existence. As such, sin rhetorically needs to name as concretely as possible the events in which life is distorted and impeded from flourishing. As the Scriptures testify to us, such lamentation is itself an act of grace in the midst of suffering. The aesthetic expressions of narratives, music, and art name concretely the reality of the sufferings of the present age. As feminist theorist Iris Marion Young suggests we must name oppression very carefully, and in our very words refuse to reduce all suffering to one term.[22] To name the oppression and suffering as carefully and as detailed as possible is to open us to the specific desires within all critical theories: the desires that these forms of oppression cease and new forms of flourishing ensue.

Thus to name sin in this fashion is also to invite the linkage of naming suffering with developing critical theories of destructiveness. For given the two conditions that José Míguez Bonino suggests, we must today speak of suffering in light of destructiveness in the world. That is suffering is the subjective referent while destructiveness is the objective referent. This challenges much of the Christian tradition at a crucial point: for sin is no longer between an individual and God with side effects on relationships with others. Nor does suffering exist in order that the good may appear, a position, it seems to me, that Wesley came dangerously close to taking in some of his writings.[23] Rather, from the unity of creation and redemption in rethinking sanctification we think of a discourse of sin that brings about emancipation from the false ideologies that objectify dominant power relations in social organization.

Rhetorically, for a feminist liberation theology in the United States I think we need to develop critical theory relating to four dimensions of destructiveness. First, we need to develop critical theories of the literal physical destruction of human beings by other humans. From analyzing the causes of women's poverties in the United States, as Pamela D. Couture has done in her book *Blessed Are the Poor?* to analyzing worldwide economic structures, to rendering the implicit notion of God in modern economic theory, as Douglas Meeks has done in his book *God the Economist*, we must develop critical theories that reveal the injustices of the present economic arrangements.[24] There are, of course, other forms of physical destructiveness: from political torture to physical abuse by women and children, to sexual exploitation and rape by lovers, friends, strangers, and political enemies. All of these forms of physical destruction must be analyzed for the false ideological assumptions they contain that mask oppressive relations of knowledge, power and interests. Christians, filled with grace, have the courage and the responsibility to speak of destructiveness as caused by injustice.

Global Destructiveness

I want especially to underscore the need to focus on global and international forces. This is of course another opportunity to link and make present the oppression in the world as well as in the US, to name a global solidarity in the midst of a critical theory. It is extremely important, theologically and politically, to realize that projections of future possibilities have to do with worldwide structures and systems. This is extremely necessary in the US since the population has little knowledge of worldwide political problems, are primarily monolinguistic, and have little contact not only with the diverse cultures in the US but with various cultures around the world.

Psychic Destructiveness

Critical theories having to do with the social causes of the high rates of addiction, mental illness, and depression in the United States must be crafted. For example, we have incredibly rich resources in the Wesleyan tradition to analyze how wealth distorts the psychic health of individual and destroys forms of human relationships. We need, in a full understanding of sin, to show that wealth is a total corruption of humanity. It is important to name this destructiveness in the United States' hegemonic culture. In the Christian tradition naming sin, it seems to me, is breaking through the denial, letting the confusion, the chaos, the dysfunction to be expressed. Sin is, in a sense, a discourse that helps us to be honest to ourselves. Working with the dominant culture in the United States means giving the opportunity for understanding that the subjective conditions created by bourgeois capitalism are not spiritually and subjectively helpful. This is why liberation theologians are quite clear that the point of theology is to create new subjects of history not to make the poor the rich, blacks into whites, or women into men.

Environmental Destructiveness

Especially in light of the unity of creation and redemption from the view point of sanctification, Christian theology should make an important contribution by forming critical theory of environmental destructiveness. This is a somewhat popular concern in the United States, but it is often approached as a way to keep the earth green for leisure or self satisfaction. A critical theory needs to link this form of destructiveness with physical, psychic, and global destructiveness. Especially because discourse of sanctification will give us alternative daily practices in our relations to other persons and the earth, it will be necessary to understand in a critical fashion how present unholy living contributes to environmental destructiveness.

We arrive at two levels: one, the lamentations of suffering—concrete expressions of suffering and destruction in the world today—and two, critical theories to examine injustice and oppression within various dimensions of destructiveness. But intermixed with these two levels, must go an analytical level that uncovers the depth order of the structure of sin as idolatry.[25] By structure I mean the hidden rules or anonymous principles that determine the formation and ongoing function of politics, language and subjectivity in cultures. Sin as idolatry is structural in the sense that it is embedded in the political practices, the everyday habits, the linguistic structures, the ways we are raised as whites, or blacks, or women or men. The depth structure of idolatry refers to the organization of social life in which women do not have rights to their bodies, in which the feminine must represent the inferior linguistic term, and in which women are raised to think of themselves in negative cultural images. Structures of sin as idolatry in global economic practices refer to specific world wide economic practices of neo-colonialism, as well as to the images of human and non-human oppression that is structured within and behind such practices.

For a feminist liberation theology I want to link together the structure of binary opposition in feminist theory with a reinterpretation of idolatry in Christian tradition. Binary opposition is the analysis that structurally the west has divided the world into two terms: men, women, black, white, the poor, the rich. These differences are structured as diametrically opposite through political, linguistic, and subjective practices.

Patricia Hill Collins, a black feminist scholar in the United States, speaks of the depth structure of this binary opposition in three steps of what she calls a complex social hierarchy.[26] First, the primacy of either/or dichotomous thinking which "characterizes people, things and ideas in terms of their difference from one another."[27] Second, in dichotomous thinking, difference is always defined in oppositional terms. Collins illustrates, "Whites and Blacks, males and females, thought and feeling are not complementary counterparts—they are fundamentally different entities related only through their definition as opposites."[28] This notion of difference as oppositional creates objectification of the opposed term, where it, the opposed term, is defined as an object that can be controlled and manipulated. Collins portrays this structuring reality:

> because oppositional dichotomies rarely represent different but equal relationships, they are inherently unstable. Tension is resolved by subordinating one half of the dichotomy to the other. Thus whites rule Blacks, men dominate women, reason is thought superior to emotion in ascertaining truth, facts supersede opinion in evaluating knowledge and subjects rule objects. The foundations of a complex social hierarchy become grounded in the interwoven concepts of either/or dichotomous thinking, oppositional difference, and objectification. With domination based on difference forming an essential underpinning for this entire system of thought, these concepts invariably imply relationships of superiority and inferiority, hierarchical bonds that mesh with political economies of race, gender and class oppression.[29]

This complex social hierarchy serves as the entry point for a contemporary reinterpretation of idolatry. In the Christian tradition idolatry is the obedience, that is the daily structured habits and practices, to false and dead gods. Gustavo Gutiérrez, defining idolatry as the acceptance of false Gods, identifies three practices of idolatry: trust and submission to something not God, ranking that which is made with human hands above humans themselves, and demanding the sacrifice of human victims.[30] As a practice that runs through all of life—from formal institutional structures to capillaries of power in common linguistic expressions—idolatry is the destruction of life's relationships, it depraves and deprives the ongoing reverence for life. Idolatry is the destruction of relations through seeking to secure and establish identity through practices that dehumanize and objectify other human beings, demanding their ongoing sacrifice to the false gods of sovereignty and consumption.

In the depth structure of binary opposition, idolatry names the distortion and destruction of relationships and the deprivation of human flourishing. The one in the dominant position cannot form relationships because his or her identity is secured only through the constant dehumanization of others. Sacrifice must be paid to the false god of sovereignty. For the "others" of history, those who are structured as the opposed term, relationships are distorted by practices, images, and institutional relations that prevent them from survival and deprive them of human flourishing. They pay the physical sacrifice rendered in idolatry; from unjust distribution of resources to the physical mutilation of women, the "others" of history are destroyed and deprived of not only survival but also flourishing.

Transforming Grace

If a Wesleyan theology of grace sets the context for developing a persuasive and transformative discourse on sin, it also provides resources and challenges us to find imaginative new ways of life. Indeed a discourse of sanctification for the United States context begins by being taken away from solely privatistic and moralistic tones and rendered as transformative possibilities for all of life. Another essay would be required for even an adequate introduction to this subject, yet the Wesleyan relation of sin and grace as not mere correctionist but transformational requires, wisely so, some concluding comments on sanctification.

Sanctification is built into the logic or we might say grammar of the Wesleyan tradition. The logic runs, I take it, something like this:

God restores us and makes us new through Jesus Christ. Redemption then is not simply reconciliation, but what I would call emancipatory transformation: emancipatory in that persons are set free from the chains of oppression and destruction, from the orders of patriarchy and poverty, from the idolatry and concupiscence of the self. But we are also transformed, and here open possibilities await us.

This is an especially important task for feminist liberationist theology in the United States for two reasons. The first reason has to do with the necessity of combining critical discourses of sin with constructive experiments of grace. Without the sanctifying moment, feminist liberation theology not only risks the problems of nihilism, but finally fails to speaks to the desires for flourishing expressed in the protests against all forms of suffering. Second, in order to be true to the movement of feminist prophetic Christianity, theology must reflect on the poetry, the new forms of lifestyle, the different ways of defining oneself, the different social and alternative patterns of life amongst women and men in this movement.[31] I will only mention three areas in which a discourse of sanctifying grace needs developing in feminist liberation theology.

Sanctifying grace might be defined as a way of living differently, a definition of grace popularized in our time by Johannes Baptist Metz.[32] Sanctifying grace has to do, as it did with Wesley, with holy living, with the practices, habits, relations, and patterns that run through our daily life. New discourses of sanctifying grace would image what these new forms of holy living might look like: new relations to our bodies, to economic possessions, to life lived in mission, to prayer as a performative activity of Jesus' dangerous memory in the world.

Sanctifying grace is life within community. Wesley, with his societies, certainly had a keen insight about the necessity and role of community for holy living and the Wesleyan tradition has often continued, in a variety of ways, this insight. Yet it is not clear in the United States what exactly community will mean in a society with radical and rapid transience, with increasing levels of multi-cultural-ism, and with changed patterns of family life.[33] Could a discourse of sanctifying grace develop images and practices of community that not only addresses these changing needs but also forms the partici-pants in patterns of openness for global solidarity rather than, as is too often the case with community formation, structures of closure to all outside the boundaries of that particular community? One of the great mission fields for the churches in the United States is to develop new forms of community as places in which persons can confront sin, where they can receive support, where persons can experiment with new forms of relationships.

Finally, sanctifying grace presents a poetics of hope to the larger culture, a manifestation of what life can be, must be, is to be in our situation. In the logic of sanctification, even the most desperate sinner can be moved onto perfection. Perhaps that logic today means that even the most idolatrous structures of life in the United States can be transformed through justice into structures which nourish instead of destroy flourishing. But if this is so, and the logic of Christianity compels me to accept this as the case, then what does this transformation look like? Can the church in the United States serve the culture and the world by giving a vision of God's reign in this concrete time and place, by awakening imaginations to dream, by birthing a *telos* of life and freedom for all of our lives?

Conclusion

I realize that I have not offered a discourse on sin applicable to all situations. Within the tenets of liberation theology, I must speak out of and to my own context, yet always in dialogue with the oppressed of all nations. But perhaps I have opened up an arena for conversation for all of us in our own local contexts: What is the relation of sin and grace today in our world? How is the Spirit of the Lord upon us as Wesleyan theologians? Anointed in the Spirit, how do we announce grace, denounce sin, and yet again announce grace in the world in which we live?

CHAPTER 6

Proclaiming Christ in All His Offices: Priest, Prophet, and Potentate

DAVID LOWES WATSON

Introduction

It was a bold step in the early 1980s to incorporate a working group on evangelism into the Seventh Oxford Institute of Methodist Theological Studies. At that time, evangelism, albeit a missional and programmatic emphasis of the church, was still a fledgling discipline of practical theology, acknowledged to some extent by missiologists, but by and large disdained by the established guilds of the religious academy.[1] The progress that has been made in the past ten years, at least from a Methodist perspective, is due in no small measure to these Institutes, which have exemplified a theological diversity and collegiality all too rare in the field of evangelistic studies, and therefore all the more welcome and vital. For this, a profound word of gratitude is owed to the steering committees who have shaped these agendas, and especially the chair persons: Brian E. Beck and M. Douglas Meeks, who represent the transatlantic taproots of our Methodist traditions; and Nora Q. Boots and Bishop Emilio J. M. de Carvalho, who represent the family of Methodism worldwide, a family now very much extended.

The decision to give evangelism a distinctive role in these Institutes was not only bold, but initially quite controversial. At best, it was argued, a focus on mission, and world mission at that, would be more appropriate. Yet the particularity of evangelism has proved at each Institute to have fostered at once an inclusive and a concrete agenda, complementing the theoretical investigations of the more academic disciplines.[2]

The Role of Evangelistic Studies

There are three additional and pressing reasons for having evangelism as a component of these Institutes.

Theological

The first is that the evangelistic outreach of the church requires serious theological reflection in order to sustain its faithfulness and authenticity. A good illustration of this was provided by the recent General Conference of The United Methodist Church. In one of the legislative committees there was a petition to be considered, advocating the right of military chaplains to carry firearms.[3] The petition was rejected, and the policy of the church unanimously affirmed, namely, that chaplains functioning as clergy should not be armed. One observer at the back of the room feigned disappointment at the outcome. "How unfortunate," he remarked. "I was just beginning to see the possibilities for a whole new method of evangelism with side-arms as a last resort!"

The observer was joking, of course. And we might share in the joke, were it not for the fact that the year was 1992, and that sidearms, to say nothing of other manifestations of military force, were by no means a last resort in evangelizing much of the so-called "New World." There were exceptions, as Justo González has reminded us in a poignant and timely article.[4] But by and large, Christian evangelism in Latin America, and indeed worldwide across the centuries, has relied on every imaginable method of coercion in order to further the kingdom of God and, as often as not, to aggrandize the church. Moreover, it is a much smaller step than it might seem to move from such blatant coercions to the more subtle, and sometimes not so subtle, persuasions and communication techniques of our own day and age. For in either instance, the evangelistic error is weighty: an unwillingness to trust in the power of the gospel to further God's work of salvation in God's own way and, of particular significance for us in an age of instant gratification, in God's own time.

Besides which, and ultimately of far greater importance, whenever human objectives and human strategies substitute for faithful discipleship in implementing the mission of God, be it through evangelism or any other ministry, be it with a view to changing persons or systems, the first and greatest casualty is always the grace of God, the supreme irony being that the very grace of God permits

114

these aberrations in the first place.[5] However concerned we might be for the homecoming of the family of God, however energized we might be for the fulfillment of the reign of God, unless we undertake rigorous and ongoing theological reflection as a necessary concomitant of evangelistic outreach, we are likely to get it terribly, terribly wrong.

Historiographical

The second pressing reason for having evangelism as an integral feature of the Oxford Institutes is historiographical. These are gatherings devoted to Methodist theological studies; and historically Methodism has been nothing if not an evangelistic movement and, though more arguably, an evangelistic church. At the 1987 Institute, the working group on evangelism made at least a token visit to some neighboring outreach ministries, so as not to be closeted in an Oxford college for the entire ten days—something that the early Methodists would have found both curious and incongruous: curious, in that a concentration of knowledge and vital piety such as this would have struck them as bound to overflow with good news to share with someone, somehow, some of the time; incongruous, in that the nickname "Methodist" stuck with these Oxford men and their spiritual progeny precisely because their lifestyle ran counter to much of the contemporary Oxford scene, rather than the mixture of awe and enchantment that tends to mark our collective sojourn in Oxford. Historiographical links with our forebears might well remind us, most especially when our attentions are focused on the poor, that Methodist theological studies, properly so-called, can never be purely, nor even primarily, an academic exercise.

Contextual

The third reason is more contextual. It is generally agreed that we are at a critical moment in human history, occasioned in part by the warfare and genocide of this century, in part by the present political uncertainty and economic disparity of the planet, but also, in larger measure than has yet been acknowledged, by the quantum leap in self-awareness galvanized by the vista of an unexplored universe and the photographed modesty of our place in it. The question is, will the church recognize this as one of God's *kairoi*— what George Hunter has described as "a rising opportunity more vast than anything the Church dared pray for"?[6]

Inasmuch as the gospel is the distinctive face we present to the world, it will be the substance and the form of our evangelism that determines the answer to this question. For the church has no monopoly on goodness, no monopoly on justice, no monopoly on faith, hope, or love, and most assuredly no monopoly on grace. The only thing unique about the church is the gospel. We alone can announce to the world with assurance and authority that Christ has died, Christ is risen, and Christ will come again. As for the rest of our life and mission, we would do well to accept with global good manners that God has many other servants, and that we accordingly have many other colleagues whose expectations are likewise those of God's *shalom*. Our particular privilege is to know the One who will preside over this universal reign of justice, love, and peace. Our particular responsibility is to let the world know, as clearly and as often as we can, what is God's ultimate design for this corner of creation. As M. Douglas Meeks has reminded us:

> Things are changing in the Methodist household. . . . In the midst of the change we should be aware that God is a strange housebuilder of a strange house. It is a resurrection household that God is struggling to build, a household in which we shall all be able to dance, without our inhibitions and our stiff joints. But God will call the tune. In the resurrection household all the household rules get changed.[7]

The Methodist traditions offer us distinct advantages in forging such an evangelism. In the first place, John Wesley himself was an evangelist *par excellence*, not only in his understanding of God's universal grace, not only in his driving concern to reach as many as possible with the good news of salvation in Jesus Christ, but also in his meticulous grounding of the gospel in the scriptures and teachings of the church. Then there are the countless men and women through whom Methodism impacted both sides of the Atlantic, not so much in Wesley's lifetime as in the nineteenth century, when ecclesial identity brought numerical growth, and resultant evangelistic tensions from which we still have much to learn. Added to which there is now the world Methodist family of churches, whose urgent task in the coming years must be to watch over their parent churches in love.

116

Preliminary Disencumbrances

Before proceeding to the substance of this evangelism, however, it will be important to relieve the word of a number of theological and ecclesial encumbrances which for long enough have handicapped its function as a ministry of the church.

Evangelism and Church Membership

First, it is imperative that we distinguish clearly between evangelism and church membership recruitment. We are now beyond the stage of conceptual or semantic argument; the issues are profoundly soteriological and eschatological.[8] The false triumphalisms and unnecessary defeatisms that result when this distinction is not made are a major pastoral and missional impediment, yet this is how we continue to evaluate much of our evangelism. Significantly, laity are much less inclined than clergy to adopt such an inappropriate criterion for the life and mission of their congregations.

This is not to deny the importance of church membership in relation to evangelism. Indeed, in non-Christian cultures it is the immediate corollary of evangelism, and in the post-Christendom cultures of the Western world, membership recruitment remains a vital and distinctive ministry of the church in its own right. Moreover, as William J. Abraham has cogently argued, not to link evangelism with the nurture and instruction of Christian catechesis is tantamount to soteriological and eschatological irresponsibility.[9] The point, however, is not the ordering of priorities, but distinction and clarity of purpose. For when the ministry of evangelism is not sufficiently distinguished from issues of church membership, the outcome is not only pastoral ecclesiocentrism, but the neglect of much evangelism that is scripturally mandated.

Evangelism and Evangelicalism

Another present encumbrance is that evangelism carries more than its fair share of the polemics associated with what has broadly come to be known as the evangelical agenda of the church. This is not the place to rehearse longstanding theological disputes, not least because few of the old labels remain serviceable. Liberalism, mainline Protestantism, fundamentalism, and even evangelicalism, have become far more diverse than their original connotations, to say nothing of the wealth of liberation and contextual theologies now enriching the world church.[10] Yet the basic issues between evangelicals and non-evangelicals are still deep. They concern a wide range of theological, biblical, historical, ethical, and pastoral faith and practice. Even if they are rarely made explicit, they are quickly apparent at any representative ecclesial gathering.[11]

It is in the area of evangelism, however, that they presently seem to be focused, indeed, one might go so far as to say unloaded. The result is that, in much of the Methodist family of churches, evangelism has become a partisan ministry. While not denying the relevance and necessity of working through these theological issues, it is time to spread the load more fairly, and not to identify them so heavily with this particular ministry. If we are to forge an evangelism that is responsive to God's *kairos*, those who lead us in its practice must allow God's Spirit to move freely through honest and collegial Christian dialogue without drawing sectarian lines of defense around particular ecclesiologies, particular eschatologies, particular soteriologies, and above all, particular spiritual gifts and faith experiences.

The Cart Before the Horse

Most especially is this collegiality important in that the pressing need today in evangelism is for a reclarification of the gospel; and this means taking the time for full and weighty biblical and theological reflection. Contextual resources we have in abundance. Indeed, therein lies a major problem: it is a perennial failing of evangelists to put the cart before the horse. Instead of focusing on the pristine task of telling the world what we have been told, we seek to actualize predetermined results. The New Testament is very clear that while there is a sense in which fields can be "ripe for harvesting" (John 4:35), there is also a sense in which premature harvesting is eschatologically presumptuous and soteriologically disruptive (Matt 13:24-30). Yet the premise of so many of our evangelistic models and strategies is to begin with the desired results, and then work backwards to find the most effective methods for their realization. At a personal level, the objective is usually conversion, with a signal disregard of the scriptural admonitions concerning the divine prerogatives of grace. At a systemic level, the mysteries of God's long, slow victory in Christ are often subsumed by perceived exigencies of quickened social change.

The Offices of Christ

So to the title of this essay, which is borrowed in part from an essay by Douglas W. Waruta in a very stimulating volume, *Faces of Jesus in Africa*.[12] The writers in this collection look at Jesus from various African perspectives, thereby reminding us, especially those of us in the West, that the multiple countenance of Jesus is at once the universality and particularity of an incarnational gospel. The essays view him as healer, as master of initiation, as liberator, chief, ancestor, and elder brother. Six women find in him their strength, their protector from evil, the revealer of their true identity, their model, helper, and teacher, their closest friend, and the core of their life. The essays are grace-filled and vibrant. As Waruta puts it:

> Other people may say a thousand things as to who Jesus is; it will never suffice, however, for the disciples of Christ to mimic the confessions of others, no matter how valid.[13]

Even so, the threefold designation of priest, prophet, and potentate will be well known to all who are versed in Christian tradition, save perhaps the title of "potentate" which, with an African sense of humor as well as context, Douglas Waruta takes from the King James version of 1 Timothy 6:15. The NRSV places us on more familiar ground: "the blessed and only Sovereign, the King of kings and Lord of lords."

The Work of Christ

Waruta argues on the one hand that these Christological designations sit well with African history and culture, but on the other hand that "the Western wing of the church, while acknowledging the threefold office, has also tended to dwell too much on the person of Christ rather than the work of Christ."[14] This is of course something our colleagues from Latin America have been telling us for quite some time, but which evangelists in the Western church have been very slow to grasp. Indeed, rather than focus on the work of Christ as the necessary complement to his person, we have tended to consign this aspect of the gospel to our pastoral colleagues, thus causing a persistent divide between evangelism and much of the servant work of the church, to the mutual impoverishment of a great many ministries. As Mortimer Arias has recently argued, at the center of our mission is an incarnational Christology, involving both the person and the work of Jesus.[15] Both are evangelistic no less than pastoral imperatives, and a proper tension between the two must be at the heart of any theological quest to tradition the gospel for our time.

Law and Grace: Faith and Works

Significantly, this is also the emphasis in a series of sermons by John Wesley where we find the same three-fold designation for Jesus. The sermons were published in the early 1750s, and focus on the relatedness of law and grace, of faith and works.[16] The law may seem an unusual *locus* for an evangelistic investigation, but in fact these sermons point us in precisely the direction we need to take today. The tension between faith and works had become an issue for Wesley very soon after Aldersgate Street, and while his concern to preach salvation by grace alone through faith alone remained central, and while, as Albert Outler notes, "the most patent danger in Wesley's delicate balancing of faith alone and holy living was its possible tilt towards moralism," by the time he penned these essays, "the opposite extreme, antinomianism, was already a clear and present danger among Methodists."[17] The key passage comes in the third sermon, "The Law Established Through Faith, Discourse II":

> It is our part thus to 'preach Christ' by preaching all things whatsoever he hath revealed. We may indeed, without blame, yea, and with a particular blessing from God, declare the love of our Lord Jesus Christ. We may speak in a more especial manner of 'the Lord our righteousness'. We may expatiate upon the grace 'of God in Christ, reconciling the world unto himself'. We may, at proper opportunities, dwell upon his praise, as bearing 'the iniquities of us all', as 'wounded for our transgressions' and 'bruised for our iniquities', that 'by his stripes we might be healed'. But still we should not 'preach Christ' according to his word if we were wholly to confine ourselves to this. We are not ourselves clear before God unless we proclaim him in all his offices . . . not only as our great 'High Priest' . . . reconciling us to God by his blood', and 'ever living to make intercession for us'; but likewise as the Prophet of the Lord, 'who of God is made unto us wisdom', who . . . 'is with us always, guiding us into all truth'; yea, and as remaining a King for ever, as giving laws to all whom he has bought with his blood . . . until he hath utterly cast out all sin, and 'brought in everlasting righteousness.'[18]

Christ as Priest Only

The evangelistic significance of this passage, and of the three sermons as a whole, is that in the prevailing mode of our evangelism today we do not proclaim Christ in all his offices, but predominantly, indeed, often exclusively, as priest. Thus, as we have noted, the prophetic and sovereign offices are viewed as belonging to other areas of mission and ministry—areas that can always be taken care of later once a person has been brought to repentance and conversion. This, however, is a very questionable assumption. To proclaim Christ only as priest is to adopt a very truncated gospel; and the danger of evangelizing with a truncated gospel is that the Christ who is presented evangelistically is very likely to be the Christ who shapes the remainder of a person's Christian life. First impressions count for a very great deal, and when persons are introduced to Christian discipleship primarily through its benefits, it is difficult, markedly difficult, to introduce them to its obligations at a later date.

The "Main Pillar" of Antinomianism

The word for this has a long history in the church, and Wesley confronts it directly in these sermons. Arguing against the concept that faith supersedes holiness,[19] he identifies the "main pillar" of antinomianism:

> Nay, but does not St. Paul expressly say, "Unto him that worketh not, but believeth on him that justifieth the ungodly, his faith is counted for righteousness"? And does it not follow from hence that faith is to a believer in the room, in the place, of righteousness? But if faith is in the room of righteousness or holiness, what need is there of this too?[20]

We allow, answers Wesley, that God justifies the ungodly by faith alone, without any goodness or righteousness preceding, and that their faith is counted for righteousness. However, this is for *preceding* righteousness, not *subsequent* righteousness. The teaching of Paul is that there is no righteousness *before* faith, but not that there is no righteousness *after* it. "He does assert holiness cannot *precede* purification; but not that it need not *follow* it."[21] Wesley proceeds to make the point even more succinctly: "Shall we be less obedient to God from filial love than we were from servile fear?"[22] "Is love a less powerful motive than fear? If not, let it be an invariable rule, 'I will

121

do nothing now I am *under grace* which I durst not have done when *under the law.' "*[23]

Antinomianism Alive and Well

The issue is not whether we are saved by grace alone through faith alone. That remains the cornerstone of the gospel. Wesley's question rather is, What kind of faith? If, in our evangelism, we present a message only of forgiveness and reconciliation, we plant the seeds of antinomianism; and today, in so much of the Western church, the seeds have proved to be of a very resilient strain. Of course, we disguise it with a multiplicity of churchly programs and ministries, but it certainly is alive and well. In its most popular form, it propagates the Christian life as a relationship with God, accomplished for us by a Christ who suffered and died at a conveniently remote time and place in history; a relationship so secure and yet so free that discipleship becomes merely a matter of following one's instincts, pursuing one's preferences and, in response to the occasional twinge of conscience, indulging in minor generosities out of major resources. Discipleship becomes the exercise of personal options that can be worked out with Jesus on a purely individual basis, in short, a Christian lifestyle fraught with the multifarious ingenuities of self-deception.

Which Jesus?

So the questions persists: Which Jesus? Jesus the priest, who atones for our sins and those of the world (Rom 5:8-11; Heb 6:20)? Or Jesus the prophet, in the tradition of Isaiah (Luke 2:76-79; 4:18-19)? Or Jesus the potentate, outraged by the persistent neglect of his little ones (Matt 25:31-46)? This is especially the question for those of us in the relatively affluent parts of the world. For when we proclaim Christ as priest to the neglect of his prophetic and sovereign offices, we devalue even his priestly work. To suggest that Christ died for character flaws that can be addressed by any competent counselor is an obscenity. Only a fraction of our sins are personal. By far the greater part are sins of neglect, sins of default, our social sin, our systemic sin, our economic sin. For these sins Christ died, and continues to die. For these sins Christ atoned, and continues to atone. Horrendous though the Los Angeles riots might have been, while

122

some fifty lives were lost in one North American city, fifty thousand continued to die each day throughout the world from hunger or hunger-related diseases.

As long as evangelism presents a gospel centered on the need for personal salvation, individuals will acquire a faith that focuses on maximum benefits with minimal obligations, and we will change the costly work of Christ's atonement into the pragmatic transaction of a salvific contract. The scandal of this kind of evangelism is our blindness to the extent to which it has been incorporated into Western individualism, narcissism, consumerism, and hedonism.

History and Incarnation

Emilio Castro states the issue well:

> In the infancy narratives we rejoice in the celebration of the coming of the Son of God, but we forget that the soldiers sent by Herod into Bethlehem are there to remind us of the brutality of the world in which we live. Jesus Christ died for us, but we forget that before he died, many children died for him. That is the interplay between the historical and the incarnational. So he took the road to Egypt as a political refugee. This historical dimension has come as a cry, challenging us to recognize that we have tamed Christ. By concentrating on the individual, the personal problem of sin, we have forgotten the actual historical struggle of Christ with historical sin and death manifested in the oppression of the poor and downtrodden of the earth.[24]

President Jimmy Carter made the same point incisively in an address he gave to the Academy for Evangelism in 1987:

> I will have a group of men my age in a Sunday School class and see them sit around, fervent Christians, dedicated Christians, enjoying the harmony and the fellowship of a community of various similar souls. Thanksgiving rolls around, and they say, Why don't we do something of a generous nature? Let us take up a collection and we will buy food, turkeys, etc. We will take this to some poor families and help them have a nice Thanksgiving. The next question is, who knows a poor family? Generally the answer is, nobody in this class knows a poor family. . . . I think ministers ought to demand as a measure of character and achievement and status from their congregation, an active reaching out.[25]

123

Christ in Full Regalia

This would be much less a problem if the Christ we presented in our evangelism was in full regalia, so to speak, and if the salvation offered in our gospel came with the conditions that Jesus clearly attached to it: not pre-conditions, but *post*-conditions. As Wesley stipulated in the General Rules of 1743, "the only condition previously required" in those who wished to be Methodists was "a desire to flee from the wrath to come, to be saved from their sins."[26] But for those who wished to remain as members, it was expected that they should "continue to evidence their desire of salvation"[27] by practicing some very specific and straightforward rules, rules which, tellingly, are often resisted vigorously today by those who have strong faith in their savior, but a personalized and spiritualized discipleship.

Christ as Prophet

When we turn to Christ as prophet, we come to what in many ways is the cutting edge of evangelism today. Wesley describes Christ in this office as "the Prophet of the Lord, 'who of God is made unto us wisdom', who by his word and his Spirit 'is with us always', 'guiding us unto all truth.'"[28] This links us meaningfully to the prophetic traditions of the Old Testament where, as Bruce Birch has explained, the message was "always centered in the character and will of God. . . . The prophets did not speak their own word to Israel, but spoke as the representatives of Yahweh, mediating a divine word to Israel."[29] Moreover, precisely because their message was directed to the people of God, it was "closely related to the time in which it was proclaimed and for which it was intended."[30]

A Personalized Christ

It is here that the form and the substance of our evangelism require a whole new dimension. We have a wealth of contextual studies that give us insights into cultures throughout the world, into social and anthropological sensitivities, but which by and large do not ask the same questions of the message we proclaim.[31] All too often the Christ of our gospel remains personalized: intimate with some, but uninvolved in the ongoing and unfolding work of God's salvation elsewhere. And when this happens, the Holy Spirit is likewise domesticated, available with special gifts on application from those who have made the right choice and exercised their salvific option. Little wonder that the awesome working of God in human history in recent years has left much of the church bemused on the sidelines.

The prophetic office of Jesus Christ is critical to the gospel, and by neglecting to give it equal emphasis with his priestly and sovereign work, not only does a great deal of our evangelism remain unattended, but the evangelism we do undertake is restricted to those who can be reached in a personal way. Once again Douglas Waruta speaks to the issue:

> [In Africa] prophets are special persons in that they are the leaders of their communities in matters both political and religious. . . . [Their role is] not restricted to the religious aspects of the community but also involves its social and political dimensions.[32]

The Universal Christ

In other words, to proclaim Christ in all his offices requires an *evangel* that does not merely offer forgiveness and reconciliation, but also includes the prophetic word that Christ has for us today; not only for us as persons, but for our communities, our cities, our nations, and indeed for the whole world. This does not mean changing the person of Christ, but simply declaring who he really is. It does not mean reducing him to historical particularities, but rather ascribing to him characteristics that are properly incarnational. It is essentially a question of truth in advertising.

Not that this dimension of evangelism has been neglected. On the contrary, there has been a succession of authors pointing us in this direction.[33] But they have yet to impact the average Western congregation, and many congregations worldwide, primarily because the field of evangelistic studies has yet to forge the models and strategies to equip church members for this task. Volumes abound in how to witness to Christ and how to share one's faith, but there is a dearth of resources in how to declare the prophetic word of Christ as an integral component of evangelistic outreach. The result is that the powers and principalities of this world do not tremble when the church declares the good news of Jesus Christ. To the contrary, the church is often used as a means of political management. One of the most cynical examples in recent times is the way in which the national administrations of the United States of America in the 1980s called on the church to take up the social slack of welfare services that are the minimum responsibility of any civilized society, but which these administrations systematically dismantled.

It is not that we are lacking in role models for challenging the powers and principalities. As any number of representatives at this Institute will readily testify, to proclaim Christ as prophet no less than priest is still to risk life and limb in many countries, including the United States of America.[34] The question is the extent to which this office of Christ is made explicit in our evangelism, a sobering and often frightening prospect for many of us in the relative safety of Western congregational life and work.

The Agenda of Christ

Yet the evangelistic imperative is clear. One of the first things a person must learn about Jesus Christ is his immediate agenda; and today, no less than in his announcement in the synagogue at Nazareth, the poor are at the top of his list (Luke 4:18-19). Which means that, while the ghettos and barrios of a country such as the United States are an ever-present challenge for the evangelist, so are the places of secular power. The poor need help, not only now, but also in the long term. They need not only compassion, but also justice.

Put differently, the good news of salvation is not merely for persons, but for institutions, for systems, and for cities and nations. The healing that comes from God in Christ is for every dimension of humanity, and this will not come by individual conversions alone. History makes that clear, as do the scriptures. The prophets, including Jesus of Nazareth, called on cities and nations to repent as well as persons (Amos 5:14-17; Jonah 3:1-10; Micah 14:1-9; Matt 11:18-24).

A Prophetic Pitfall

Yet herein lies a pitfall for the prophetic evangelist, one which those of us in evangelistic studies could do much to forestall if the prophetic Christ were to be firmly on our agenda. It is what Jürgen Moltmann early identified in his work as presumptive utopianism, the desire to assist with the present agenda of Jesus Christ to the extent that we forget whose agenda it is.[35] The pitfall is subtle and seductive primarily because the most difficult aspect of Christian discipleship is to sustain a personal relationship with Christ. Ironically, in view of what we have just argued, it is much, much easier to work for Christ than to talk with him. It is much more congenial to participate in Christian community than to wrestle with Christ one-on-one. The saints who spend whole nights in prayer are not exercising a discipline nearly so much as experiencing the importunity of a priestly prophet who will not take no for an answer. The whole point of discipleship, as Frederick Herzog has explained, is to *walk* with Christ, not to avoid him.[36]

Bishop Robert Morgan of the Mississippi Area has declared that we have not only found it easier in North America to build new sanctuaries than to form Christian disciples, not only more palatable to study the Bible than to live it out, but also more appealing to engage in social action than to confront people with the challenge of Jesus Christ. The penetrating stare of Jesus Christ in the empty eyes of the starving and the downtrodden calls us to personal no less than corporate repentance.

God's Election of the Poor

One thing, however, must be said: the poor themselves manage to avoid this pitfall. In fact, they understand its seductiveness far more than those of us who attempt to theologize on their behalf, for the simple reason that the gospel raises their consciousness more keenly than any of us who attempt to raise it for them. So it was in Wesley's day, and so it is today.[37] The good news of Christ as priest is welcomed by the poor, for they are only too aware of their sin and their need for forgiveness and reconciliation. The good news of Christ as prophet is likewise readily accepted, inasmuch as they know the sufferings of the world first hand, and are more than willing to help with Christ's unfinished task. When we talk about God's preferential option for the poor, therefore, it is not so much a declaration of missional or evangelistic priority, as of divine election.

The truth of the matter is that God's deepest truths *are* grasped most readily by the poor, because they are the ones whose eyes God chooses to open. They are the ones who, lacking most worldly riches, are blessed with spiritual wealth.[38] The fact that political and religious leaders have counted on this for centuries to exercise social manipulation ultimately does nothing to lessen it—a double paradox that social historians, and especially students of the Halévy thesis, usually fail to take into account.[39] Those who work and live with the poor understand it, however, for there indeed the fields are white unto harvest.[40]

Christ as Potentate

Last, we come to Christ as potentate. Prior to the King James, or Authorized, version of the Bible, William Tyndale's translation had read "blessed and mighty," and the Geneva Bible "blessed and prince onely." Given our heightened sensitivities today, however, symbols of royalty, and masculine royalty at that, tend to be semantically impedimental and symbolically oppressive. Not to beat about the bush, none of us likes to be told what to do these days, be it by those with political power, or by those with religious authority, be they pastors, superintendents, or bishops. This is why, of course, a personalized discipleship, negotiated in convenient seclusion with Jesus, is so attractive. It allows us maximum flexibility. We should remember, therefore, that power and majesty are not only the due of Jesus Christ, but can be ascribed with total confidence to a God who exercises them with the safeguard of trinitarian collegiality.

Patriarchal Evangelism

Perhaps the chief reason why the issue of power becomes problematic for evangelism is that the field is overwhelmingly male-dominated; and while this should not constitute a problem *per se*, it does raise the interesting question of why so few women emerge today as evangelistic leaders. After all, one of the marks of early Methodism was the leadership role taken by women, first as class leaders, and then as preachers, with a brisk pace set by Susanna Wesley herself. Does their absence by and large today cause our evangelism to have a slanting of theological perspective and pastoral strategy?

Some years ago Virginia Ramey Mollenkott presented a paper at a symposium held at Perkins School of Theology in which she argued that this was precisely the state of affairs.[41] It was a foundational statement, and it remains remarkably pertinent to our thinking today. She suggested that evangelism in the North American church was in fact patently patriarchal, and offered five criteria by which it is normatively measured, criteria, we should note, that are very difficult to find in the scriptures. First, the idea that bigger is better;

that the size of a congregation is a sign of God's blessing, or at least its evangelistic effectiveness. Second, that competition is inevitable, and that as evangelists we are therefore in a win-lose situation, if not with the world, then certainly with other churches. Third, that human fulfillment stems from measurable achievements, as opposed to God's love, which is altogether unconditional. God's love affirms the dignity of every human being, regardless of accomplishments. Fourth, patriarchal evangelism implies that ordinary human living must be transcended in order to meet the standards of the gospel; which is, of course, fundamentally to misunderstand the nature of grace and conversion. While there is much about human life that most assuredly is changed by the grace of *metanoia*, the doctrine of justification declares that God accepts us just as we are, and invites us thereafter to share in a transforming friendship. Lastly, patriarchal evangelism implies that some people have more standing in God's sight than others, whereas the gospel clearly declares God's love for all. If there is preferential treatment, it is for the child who is hungry, for the prisoner who suffers, for the lonely and the abandoned. God has no other distinctions; none whatsoever.

A Limited View of Grace

Yet distinctions abound in our evangelism: the "saved" and the "unsaved," the "lost" and the "found," the "churched" and the "unchurched." We have become so caught up in the dynamics of a personal evangelism, that we have not examined the anomaly of proclaiming on the one hand that God loves the whole world, but reserving as our trump card, so to speak, the threat that God will consign to eternal perdition those who refuse to accept what we tell them. Never mind that this is a card we hope we will not have to use; never mind that we disapprove of the methods of many who do use it. The danger lies in the mindset it fosters: a thoroughly inadequate view of grace.

The criticism levelled at Mollenkott, and at some others who affirm a doctrine of universal grace, is that they are propagating universalism, a word about which a great deal is said by a great many people on the basis of very little reading. But if we subscribe to a doctrine of universal grace, something that Wesley affirmed at an early date in his field preaching,[42] then the real danger is not universalism, but rather the presumption to restrict God's grace. Of course

God's judgments remain in place for all eternity, for the Christian no less than the pagan, for the righteous no less than the sinners. But a grace that is truly universal must be proclaimed without any human qualification at all—and that means scrupulously avoiding discriminatory language or concepts that even remotely imply who is "saved" or "unsaved." Those are God's words, and God's alone. They must therefore be excised from our evangelistic vocabulary.

The Visionary Wesley

What do we put in their place? Well, we might begin with Wesley's assignation of Christ "as remaining a King for ever; as giving laws to all whom he has bought with his blood; as restoring those to the image of God whom he had first reinstated in his favor; as reigning in all believing hearts until he has 'subdued all things to himself'; until he hath utterly cast out all sin, and 'brought in everlasting righteousness.' "[43] Or we might turn to a visionary passage from the sermon he preached before Oxford University in 1744:

> But shall we not see greater things than these? Yea, greater than have been yet from the beginning of the world? Can Satan cause the truth of God to fail? Or his promises to be of none effect? . . . Suppose now the fullness of time to be come, and the prophecies to be accomplished—what a prospect is this! . . . Here is no din of arms, no 'confused noise', no 'garments rolled in blood'. 'Destructions are come to a perpetual end: wars are ceased from the earth. . . . Civil discord is at an end for evermore, and none is left either to destroy or hurt his neighbour'. Here is no oppression to 'make even the wise man mad'; no extortion to 'grind the face of the poor'; no robbery or wrong; no rapine or injustice; for all are 'content with such things as they possess'. Thus 'righteousness and peace have kissed each other'; they have 'taken root and filled the land'; righteousness flourishing out of the earth, and 'peace looking down from heaven'.[44]

It is late in his ministry, however, that we find Wesley at his most eschatologically eloquent, universal in his hope, and seasoned in his pastoral perspective.[45] Take, for example, his sermon, "The General Spread of the Gospel":

> And in every nation under heaven we may reasonably believe God will observe the same order which he hath done from the beginning of Christianity. 'They shall all know *me*,' saith the Lord, not from the greatest to the least (this is the wisdom of the world which is

130

foolishness with God) but 'from the least to the greatest,' that the praise may not be of men, but of God. Before the end even the rich shall enter the kingdom of God. Together with them will enter in the great, the noble, the honourable; yea, the rulers, the princes, the kings of the earth. Last of all the wise and learned, the men of genius, the philosophers, will be convinced that they are fools; will 'be converted and become as little children, and enter into the kingdom of God'.[46]

We must of course take note of the famous injunction that his preachers had "nothing to do but to save souls."[47] But this was in the context of a warning not to be distracted by organizational goals and objectives. It does not obviate the larger context of God's universal salvation. As Theodore Runyon has observed, the note of eschatological fulfillment in Wesley's Oxford sermon of 1744 is amplified in this 1783 sermon and others in the Second Series.[48] Moreover, Runyon suggests, it is significant that Wesley himself never used the term *ordo salutis*, and these later sermons may give us a clue as to why this was the case. For they reveal that the decisive event of conversion and the process of sanctification cannot be properly understood in a purely individualistic context. They must be seen in their organic relation to creation and kingdom. To interpret them in a more narrow way is to deprive them of their intended significance.[49]

Matriarchal Possibilities

It is this universal perspective on God's salvation that a matriarchal evangelism might help us to forge in response to God's present *kairos*. Fatherhood is all too often selective, as the biblical narratives amply illustrate; and well has it been said of the male seed that many are called, but few are chosen. By contrast, there is an inevitability to motherhood, an acceptance of the family as it is, a willingness to work with the wayward child for as long as it takes. The evangelistic question might then become, not "How many?" but "How long?" The energy of our evangelism might then be channelled, not only into persuading people to accept an invitation to the heavenly feast, but also to convincing them of the necessity of table manners.

Christ's True Power: Perseverance

For the true power of our particular potentate is in fact perseverance. God does not act irresistibly with us, explains Wesley; not "with the same ease as when 'God said, Let there be light; and there was light.'"[50] God does not take away our understanding, but enlightens and strengthens it. God does not destroy our affections, but makes them more vigorous. Least of all does God take away our liberty. Rather, assisted by God's grace, we choose, like Mary, the better part. "And in the same manner as God has converted so many to himself without destroying their liberty, he can undoubtedly convert whole nations, or the whole world. And it is as easy to him to convert a world as one individual soul."[51]

In her address to the Eighth Oxford Institute in 1987, Mercy Amba Oduyoye spoke about this kind of power:

> If I wanted to ask for the authority figure among a group of people, I would ask for the "one who looks after them." The manner of such a person would be described as confident and fearless. . . authority is assigned to or acquired by those who possess knowledge and the wisdom of experience and who speak the mind of the people. In such a situation, power and authority would have the same meaning. God in the Lord's Prayer is described as being the owner of *tumi* (power), and *Otumfo* translates to "Almighty" in Christian prayers. . . . Legitimate *tumi* is authorized. The authorization comes from the group which recognizes in the person what is needed for its well-being. Performing as an *Otumfo* would have no connotation of domination . . . Authority flows from a sense of responsibility as is evidenced in parenting and therefore nurtures toward maturity and self-determination.[52]

The Wrath and the Love of God

Here lies the bedrock of our gospel. Yes, we have faith in Christ our High Priest; and yes, we have hope in Christ our Prophet. But greater than these is the love of Christ, the One who reveals to us the power of God's parenthood. Thus, if there is to be a word of warning in our evangelism, a word of censure and judgment, let it be this: That there will indeed be a *dies irae*, a day when the pent-up anger of a God whose patience and good manners seem limitless will finally be unleashed (Rom 2:5). The little ones of this world, the downtrodden, the poor, will not be left unvindicated. The tares still grow with the wheat, but not forever (Matt 13:24-30).

Our evangelistic word of warning, therefore, is not so much the priestly admonition to repent of sin, personal and social, important though that may be, nor yet the prophetic exhortation to do justice, love kindness, and walk humbly with God, important though that may be also, but above all the royal summons to prepare for audience with a wrathful parental potentate whose children have been neglected and starved and beaten and slaughtered for millennia. On that day of God's anger, we shall all tremble for a long, long time.

Yet even with this, there is still good news. "For I am convinced," wrote Paul, "that neither death, nor life, nor angels, nor rulers, nor things present, nor things to come, nor height, nor depth, nor anything else in all creation, will be able to separate us from the love of God in Christ Jesus our Lord" (Rom 8:38-39). To which we might add, not even an evangelistically lethargic and incompetent church.

CHAPTER 7

The 500th Anniversary of The European Invasion of Abya-Yala: An Ethical and Pastoral Reflection from the Third World

VICTORIO ARAYA-GUILLÉN
Translated by Gloria Kinsler

And the LORD said, "What have you done? Listen; your brother's blood is crying out to me from the ground!" (Genesis 4:10)

Editor's Note: Abya-Yala is the name given to the American continent by the Kuna Indians of Panama. In 1977 the World Council of Indigenous Peoples chose this name for the continent as an affirmation of Indian roots and identity.

Introduction

The dawn of the third millennium confronts us with a painful historical reality of sinfulness: the holocaust of the majority of human beings—the poor of the earth. In the last few years the world has changed rapidly. There are those who say that the third millennium began with the fall of the Berlin wall (1989) and the end of the East-West confrontation.[1] Yet have the unjust conditions of death for the majority poor really changed? Are we not building a wall of silence around the death of the poor? It is revealing that at the same time that the "end of history" (Fukuyama) was announced along with the triumph of capitalism, the World Bank published the *Report on World Development 1990: Poverty*, which represents poverty as "the most urgent question of the decade."[2] The reality of one billion persons with a per capita income of less than $370 a year reveals the extent of the crisis and the tragedy. According to recent data from the United Nations, forty million persons, half of them children, die every year from hunger and malnutrition. If we were to decide to have one minute of silence for each person who died in any recent year of hunger-related causes, we would not be able to greet the arrival of the twenty-first century because our voices would still be silenced. In the Third World today we suffer as many deaths each year as during the horrors of World War II.[3] In Brazil, the eighth largest capitalist economy, four hundred thousand children less than one year old die each year. This is the equivalent to a Hiroshima atomic bomb every fifty days.[4]

These data are not cold, neutral statistics. They indicate the fundamental dilemma in the life and death of the poor. These deaths have a human face: women, children, peasants, indigenous. They are evidence of the destruction of the gift of life, a reality that is contrary to the will of God for creation. It is a situation of sin.

The threatened holocaust of the poor raises fundamental questions for the life of the church: How are we to be a community of faith in a world of injustice and death for the poor? How do we announce, by deed or word, the good news of life that comes from God (John 10:10) in the midst of this bad news of the daily death of the poor who are victims of the economic rationale imposed by the West?

Basic Presuppositions

An Attitude of Humility: Listening, Discerning, and Confessing

Given the challenges to the churches created by the magnitude of poverty in the world, we need to make a theological and pastoral response from an attitude of listening to and discerning the plight of the poor. New and important questions have arisen that impose upon the churches as never before an approach which is dominated by a willingness to search for answers. Only a humility that leads to confessing can make us able to face the death of the poor.

A Reflection "From the Underside of History"

No reflection of faith and ethical response is possible without being geographically and historically grounded. The following reflection is so based. It is not universally abstract but particular. We speak from the geography of the Third World ("The South") and from the "underside" of history.

The Historical Contradiction: Life/Death

We start with a basic fact: the universality of today's life-destroying forces. This fact confronts us with an historic dilemma: the life-death of the poor majorities of the world. We can express our basic thesis this way: The principal contradiction which presently polarizes human history in the international context is no longer the East/West tension but the life/death, a North/South contradiction. This contradiction places the countries of the South, the poor, throwaway nations, against the countries of the North, the countries of the metropolitan centers (not the peoples thereof) located in the United States, Europe, and Japan with their enormous economic, technological, cultural and military power.

The majority of all humanity, two-thirds of it, more than four billion persons, live in the South, whereas the North represents one-third of the world's population. During the hundred years between 1900 and 2000 the world's population will have grown from 1.6 billion to 6 billion. This growth occurred mainly in the South.

1492–1992: 500 Years of Conquest and Western Expansion "In the World on the Periphery"

1992 marks the fifth centenary of the conquest and evangelization of Latin America by Europe which was related to the European Renaissance mercantile expansion of the sixteenth century. "October 12, 1492 began, for Latin America and the Caribbean, an enormous Good Friday of suffering and blood that continues up to today without knowing Easter."[5]

With the western invasion of the continent, Abya-Yala underwent in a few years the largest genocide of history[6] the death of more than 70 million indigenous people, the destruction of their culture, the theft of their land, the destruction of nature, and the uprooting of millions of Africans who were enslaved by the Colonial powers. Following centuries of colonial expansion and including our present neocolonial order, a small minority of humanity has imposed its western model of society with its cultural and religious values, its political, military, economic models, its mass media, and its financial and technological power.

The Option for Life: The Defense of the Gift of Life, Especially of the Poor and of Nature

In face of this historical dilemma of life/death, the Methodist churches who have faith in the God of Life and are followers of Jesus who came to bring Good News of an abundant life must be more than ever faithful in the defense of the threatened life of the poor and the threat to nature. This faithfulness to life is not just one more task; it is an ethical and pastoral imperative. The Gospel will be Good News for the poor if it is the Good News of life.

Capital as an Economic Idol Contrary to Life

Capitalism: "Bad News for the Poor"

If the Gospel is Good News for the poor, capitalism with its economic "logic" is bad news. It is bad news because of its "logic" of economic growth and accumulation which is contrary to the life of the poor and of nature. Thus capitalism confronts the logic of life which is revealed in the Good News of the Kingdom of God. Human beings, and the poor are human, have in the Gospel a supreme value; they are sacred beings made in the image of God. Life is a gift of God who has chosen to establish justice and the right to life for victims and "the least of these." We Christians should realize that the "anti-life character of the theories and economic practices of capitalism mean an anti-gospel."[7] In the economic "logic" of capitalism, capital and the laws of the market come first. Human beings and the satisfaction of their basic needs and the right to life for all come second.

Poverty is not a subjective, individual phenomenon; it is not a product of chance; it does not fall from heaven as God's will or God's punishment. Nor is it the result of insufficient technology or natural resources. Poverty is not a neutral phenomenon or cold economic fact. It cannot be, because poverty has a human face and that face confronts us every day with the theological and ethical dilemma of the death of millions of innocent human beings.[8]

Poverty: Not a Free Gift from Heaven

Poverty is an historic, social, and economic act that has a beginning and objective causes with economic mechanisms and social subjects. It responds objectively to a process that is determined by "reason" and the will of human beings. It is a complex process that was developed from the Renaissance mercantile expansion of the sixteenth century to today's international neoliberal capitalism (the new free market economy). Within this process, thanks to unequal exchange, some countries "specialize in gaining and others in losing"[9] until today there are clearly "the losers," throw-away nations.

Capitalism and the Triumph of Exclusion

The events that in these last years have changed the world, e.g., the crisis and fall of socialism in Eastern Europe, have been proclaimed as the triumph of western capitalism, "the end of history," "the New World Order." Capitalism, in its new market economy version, with its policy of structural adjustments designed and imposed by the International Monetary Fund and the World Bank, is presented as the only possible alternative for humanity. Before these changes capitalism had to care about presenting a human face. It had to have economic policies of development so that the poor would not opt for radical change. Within the new global geopolitics, capitalism does not need to worry about reform and development policies because it is imposed as the only solution. Now capitalism is only interested in very partial reforms as functions of its immediate interests, and not for the benefit of the world in the South. The great impoverished majorities do not count. They are left in a condition of abandonment and death. As a Latin American theologian has expressed it, "The Third World is no longer even dependent, we are simply nonexistent. We go from being a dependency to being expendable. Now to be dependent seems like a privilege since the majority are condemned to oblivion and death."[10] We can no longer speak of a Third World; we are now the last world, the world of the excluded and condemned to death.

The Idolatry of Capital

Capitalism is a system of economic idolatry. Idolatry occurs when humankind deposits its faith and life in something that is not God, but a creation of its own hands, the idol.[11] The relativity of all human creation becomes a sacred absolute and the idol is given the prerogatives that only belong to God. In the economic "logic" of capitalism, the idolatry of capital occurs: when capital is given priority before human beings and the satisfaction of their basic needs or when economic laws, a human creation within social history, become an

139

end in themselves. Laws, like the Sabbath in the Biblical tradition, are a means for life. Economic laws cannot be primarily for the service of capital, but for the promotion of life. In capitalism humans beings and their needs must adapt themselves to the economic laws of the market; the market and its laws do not adapt themselves to the basic needs of the majority of human beings.

In the new capitalist market economy, the laws of the market are absolute and untouchable; they cannot be changed. They acquire a sacred character that legitimates them as the only possible road to salvation for the economic problems of society. "Outside the market there is no salvation;" there is only chaos and hell on earth. As long as capital is converted into an idol and the laws of the market are absolutized, the triumphant economic "rationality" does not respond to the right to life of the majorities. The poor are excluded, they are no longer important. Their death is not even news.

The Sacrificial Character of Capitalism

It is necessary to discern the sacrificial character of capitalism in its demand for human sacrifice. What is human sacrifice if it is not the slow or rapid death of the millions of poor in the countries of the South whose life and blood are squeezed out by national or international capital and transferred to the countries of the North in order that the sacred market remains untouchable and gives life and growth to massive capital.[12] The life of the poor and the life of nature are sacrificed as a necessary payment in order to participate in the new sacred economy: the international system of the free market. The demands laid upon the countries of the South as conditions of their access to the international market are in actuality nothing less than human sacrifice.

The clearest example of this reality is the problem of the external debt of the South. (In Latin America the debt is more than $400,000,000,000.)[13] The demand for the debtor nations to pay the interest has turned into an economic war against the poor. In order to pay the interest (in Latin America, more than $140 billion from 1982 to 1989), the governments of the South are obliged to invest less and less in basic services: health, housing, food, and work. The poor are the sacrificial victims. No real sacrifice is demanded of those truly responsible for the crisis: the international financial system for which the obligation to pay has priority over the attention to basic needs which takes second place. It is the logic of a system that is against life.

It is no accident that in Latin America at the dawn of the third millennium, at the moment of the triumph of western capitalism, we live the tragedy of "the times of cholera," a disease of the last century that has returned to stay. This reflects the profound economic and social crisis in which we live every day in the South. For this reason, from the perspective a Christian faith opposed to human sacrifice and for an ethic of life, the payment of the debt must be condemned, since it is undermining the future life of the majority of humanity and provoking a real catastrophe. "Pay or die," says a popular slogan. We want to live!

Capital: The Ferocious Beast of Our Time

To conclude this brief reflection on the importance of understanding the international capitalist system, let us turn to a word that comes from the experience of the Christian Base Communities of Brazil.[14] To denounce prophetically the bad news (dis-grace) that capitalism brings to the poor, they call capitalism the "ferocious beast" of our times. This image taken from the book of Revelation seems to us to be very useful today to point to the empire of the idol Capital, the sacred laws of the market, its absolute power and its demands for sacrifice. Without a doubt the international capitalist system is the ferocious beast that opposes the life-giving action of the God of life whose loving will for all creation is first and last.

The World's Poverty: a Challenge to the Methodist Ecclesial Tradition

A Time of Grace and Ecclesial Conversion

The 500th year celebration in the West could be a moment of grace and conversion for the Christian churches.[15] This would mean that we question and distance ourselves from the model of colonial Christianity transplanted by the West. We have to confess that during the last 500 years the kind of evangelical practice that has developed from the North has had a very close relationship with Western expansion with its power to dominate, with its eagerness for the accumulation of wealth, and its supposed racial superiority. In this expansion the name of God has been manipulated and transformed into a symbol of power, order, law, and wealth. That is very different from the "God who listens to the cry of the victims" (Exod 2:24; 3:7).

141

Since 1492 western Christianity has been proud to be in the center of the world with its political, economic, cultural, military, and technological domination. Because of this power wielded by the West, the life of the peoples of the South and the life of nature have been violated and destroyed.[16] If we Christians want to be faithful to the Spirit of Jesus in this time of grace we must confess the sin of the European invasion of Abya-Yala and the death of millions of innocent human beings and live, celebrate, and announce the Good News for the poor from a perspective of service and not from power.

The Evangelizing Potential of the Poor

Commitment to the poor and the rise of the Christian Base Communities have helped the churches in Latin America to discover "the evangelizing potential of the poor." The poor have questioned the churches, calling them to conversion and challenging them to make real and visible the signs of the Kingdom.[17] The historical experience of the life of the poor has deeply challenged the way in which we read the Bible, understand the history of the church, define our pastoral ministry, and announce the Good News within the framework of western epistemology and axiology, that is to say, "from above," from the dominant culture. We have not respected or listened to the "world of the other," because it does not have anything to do with "my world." In Latin America we speak a lot of the "logic of life." From that understanding we are re-reading the Bible to rediscover the primordial correlation God/life as central to the history of Salvation.[18]

Discovering the Mystery of Loving God as the God of Life

The God of the Bible is revealed as the God of Life. It is God's saving will that all human beings have life. Because of this, God generates and defends the right to life for all creation. Faith in the biblical God is faith in a living God. There is a unity between being truly God and giving life. Idols and false gods offer life but really lead to death.

To believe in the God of Life is to believe that God's primordial design is for human beings to have life. There can be no faith in God without the deep conviction of the absolute supremacy of life over death. A denial of life is a rejection of the God of Life. To believe in the God of Life is to believe that the nature of sin emerges in its inmost essence as a force of death. Sin is the denial of God by the annihilation of human life. Faith in the God of Life must come through the demand that life be bestowed now on the poor majorities who die in history.

To say life is to say concrete, material life: work, land, housing, bread, health, education, and natural resources.[19] Basic necessities are the minimal corporal realities without which there is no human life with freedom and dignity. These needs respond to an ethical imperative but are also economic. The defense of concrete human life is an ethical and economic imperative but also an expression of spirituality, because work and bread are also realities that God sees as necessary for the development of human life. According to the Bible the spiritual is never opposed to the material created by God. The contradiction is between the spiritual and an individualism that accumulates material goods and wealth for its own ends. In the tradition of the Ancient Church it was Ireneas of Lyon who said, *gloria Dei, vivens homo*: God's glory is a living human being. Oscar Romero, Salvadorean bishop and martyr, concretized this truth most meaningfully: "Early Christians used to say *gloria Dei, vivens homo*. We could make this more concrete by saying *gloria Dei, vivens pauper*: The glory of God is the living poor human being."[20]

A Prophetic Reading

Discerning the signs of the time is a matter of discerning idolatry as the main sin of our times. It is necessary to discern the profound idolatry at the root of the anti-life logic of the dominant economic system.[21] In a society like ours in the final days of the scientific and technological twentieth century, the theme of idolatry may seem to refer only to ancient or primitive religions. Nevertheless, the Bible reminds us constantly that we human beings invent false gods or idols, place our confidence in them, and then submit ourselves to their demands.

Everyday the capitalist system shows itself to be an idol. Because of the system's trust in the idol capital, it promotes an Olympus of idols and false gods. These gods have concrete names, such as, "Western Christianity," "free market," "accumulation of capital," "maximum profit," "structural adjustment," "economic growth," and "national security." Everywhere their worshippers comply with their demands.

The idols are at the service of power and the oppression of human beings. Their demand for obedience is absolute. Although their promises are order, liberty, happiness, well-being, power, and consumption, in reality they do not lead to life but death, especially for the poor and creation. These idols of death, like the ancient god Moloch, demand victims and blood. Hence, the holocaust of the poor, death by sacrifice of millions of innocent human beings, the majority being children. What does this discernment between the true God and the false gods of the economic system imply for the ethical-pastoral task?

The opposite of a faith in the God of Life is not atheism or secularism as a negation of the existence of God. Faith in the true God is confronted with the dominant idols and idolatries. We are involved in a real struggle between the God of life and the idols of death. For the believer this is not a doctrinal or an apologetic struggle but a problem of life or death.

Idolatry is an expression of a profound perversion of the sense of God, a deformation of God's image. When the God of Life is denied as father/mother, when God is denied as the giver of life, it becomes possible to legitimate or ignore the death of the other. When God is denied as love, tenderness, and affection, we cannot listen or be in active solidarity with the victims.

This raises a real challenge to our faith in obedience to God. Faith in the God of Life cannot be lived if not in contradiction to the idols of death. The historic reality of death as it is expressed in exclusion, injustice, and lack of solidarity is against the saving will of God.

To be a believer and to be able to proclaim the God of Life we must abandon the idols of death: "We cannot serve two masters." Today, as in the case of the first Christians, a peculiar form of "atheism" is needed for faith. We need to be atheists of false gods, the gods of death. In words of the Gospel: We cannot serve at the same time the God of Life and the idols of death (cf. Matt 6:24). In the life of the church we need to rediscover the central element of the prophets: the knowledge and worship of the true God is united with the practice of justice, mercy and the defense of the right to life (cf. Jer 22:13-16; Mic 6:8). It is this which differentiates faith in God from all idolatrous practices.

Dimensions of Ecclesial Praxis

We may speak of three dimensions of ecclesial practice: hearing, accepting, and serving the poor. (1) *Hearing the poor* is the church's first challenge. The victims of poverty "cry for help" (Exod 2:23). Their death speaks loudly. Who listens to them? To listen to the cry of the poor is to allow them to challenge us, however hard that might be. Listening is one of the characteristics of God's solidarity with the poor. God as Word, above all others, knows to listen; God "inclines his ear" (Ps 17:6). The cry of the poor touched the heart of God (cf. Pss 34:7; 69:34). God rescues the poor from oppression and violence; their lives are precious to Him (Ps 72:14).

(2) *Accepting the poor* means that the church recognizes and opens itself to the "others" as persons of value, as children of God, for their contribution to the church. Because of capitalism's "logic" of exclusion they have never been recognized as persons, as subjects. It is the recognition of the other that prevents their exclusion and death. A concern for the poor challenges the churches to realize the Abrahamic experience of leaving home, of the Exodus journey, of the necessity of leaving our own circle toward the "other," who is not recognized by the "logic" of domination.

(3) *Serving the poor* means the church in active solidarity defending threatened life in a world where compassion and mercy are anti-value for the legal empire imposed by the market economy. It means going "directly to the poor." The announcement of the Good News of life produces concrete practice: the practice of love, of mercy, of compassion; the vital syntheses between the Gospel and life, faith and works. The evangelical parable of the "good Samaritan" shows us our primary task in active solidarity: Today "the fallen and the half dead" are the victims of the unjust international economic order.

Conclusion

There are many in our society and in the churches who are tired of speaking about the poor. It is important to remember that today it is the majority of humankind that are forced to suffer and die because they are poor. In conclusion let us lift up two important aspects.

First is the question of defeating "the scandal's temptation." The Beatitudes of the Gospel are not revealed to those who do not see the scandal in the messianic practice of Jesus in the service of the reign of God promised to the poor (cf. Matt 11:1-6). For Jesus the poor are real historical persons.[22] The poor are those who have real needs (hunger, thirst), all those who are weighed down under a heavy burden. They are those who are excluded socially: sinners, tax collectors, prostitutes, and the little ones who are not offered the hope of salvation but exclusion and condemnation by official religion. The Good News is different: "Blessed are you who are poor, for yours is the kingdom of God" (Luke 6:20, cf. Pss 69:32-33; 72:4, 12-14; 103:6; 146:7-9).

The second concern is working with the Spirit's power for "Good News" as "good reality." The Good News to the poor will only be credible if it is converted into a good reality that defends and maintains the life of the poor and all creation. The Good News runs the risk of being forgotten because of "the sin of the world." It is up to us to make the Good News a reality.

Faced with this threat the life of the poor and that of nature, we may speak of a five-fold urgency: (1) To build an ethic from a ministry of solidarity with biblical and Wesleyan roots that affirms life as the supreme gift of God for all creation and to struggle against the idols of power and money that condemn to death the poor and creation. (2) To promote unity and dialogue in the churches to support prophetic voices and actions of resistance in defense of life. (3) To create spaces in the life of the church for discussion about the challenge of the poor and of the importance of supporting all efforts toward economic policies that have human beings and the satisfaction of their basic needs as a priority. (4) To confront the dilemma life/death with the constructive participation of all is necessary, believers or not. But for the churches, it is important that they support the participation of new social subjects: women, peasants, indigenous peoples, blacks, ecological and human rights movements, each with their specific struggle. (5) To contribute from our faith in the God of Life to efforts to keep alive an active "hope against hope."

These words from the Kingston Theological-Pastoral Declaration (1990) sum up the task before us:

> Challenged by the unbearable suffering of the most poor and recovering the prophetic vocation of the Christian faith . . . we must come out from the closed doors of our mental structures, abandon our church buildings and become pilgrims on the way. . . . To be with Jesus the Christ is to give testimony to his resurrection in the midst of the negation of life for the least of these, our brothers and sisters. . . . Our trust in the Lord will keep us from fainting and give us strength to be bearers of hope; He accompanies us to the end of time (cf. Matt 29:30).[23]

CHAPTER 8

Charles Wesley and the Poor

S T KIMBROUGH, JR.

Introduction

The Introduction to *Sermons by the Late Rev. Charles Wesley, A.M.* (1816), according to tradition written by Charles's wife Sarah, says that "John affectionately discharged the social duties, but Charles seemed formed by nature to repose in the bosom of his family."[1] Thus was established, at least in part, the basis for the prevalent generalization that John was the socially engaged brother and Charles the socially less-engaged, poet-hymn writer, and family man.

Charles's *Journal*, letters, sermons, and even his hymns paint a somewhat different picture. However, let it be clear from the outset that no attempt to romanticize Charles's contribution to the achievement of social justice in eighteenth-century England will approach reality. John and Charles were different in this matter as in many others. While they have often been viewed as almost identical "twins" in thought and deed, some have drawn the contrasts sharply. Frank Whaling has claimed that "when we examine the brothers within the broader Methodist context, their dissimilarities pale into significance beside the basic unity of their hearts and minds."[2] In contrast, Erik Routley says this of John and Charles:

> They were in some ways complementary; yet, in fact, they saw less of one another than brothers engaged in such work as theirs might be expected to do, and their approach to religion and life differed in matters so fundamental that open disagreement between them was not only possible, but was probably as infrequent as it was only because they spent so little of their time in company.[3]

In addressing the subject of Charles Wesley and the poor, what is there to be said about Charles that cannot be said of John? Does

Charles make a contribution to this subject that is uniquely his own? Perhaps the uniqueness of his contribution lies not so much in differences of ethical and theological views and practice, but in the way he opened for the church to remember its responsibility to the dispossessed of the earth.

The description of the social engagement of the brothers in the Introduction to the 1816 volume of sermons mentioned above is important for understanding the background and influences on Charles. Samuel, the eldest brother, had a tremendous impact on the young Charles, especially at Westminster School, where he was an Usher when Charles arrived there as a young scholar. The influence of his churchmanship, scholarship, and poetry on Charles are well known. Charles was also aware that "the infirmary for the sick and poor at Westminster was first projected by him (Samuel), and his strenuous endeavours eminently promoted its success."[4]

It is common knowledge that the small group of students at Oxford which included Charles and John followed in Samuel's footsteps, so to speak, in a concern for others—visiting the sick and those in workhouses and prisons, establishing a charity school, and instructing the uneducated poor. The outcasts of society were objects of their passion, even before "conversion."

Certainly the involvement with the dispossessed prisoners and poor in the Colony of Georgia, the encounter with the horrors of slavery (the cruelties of which Charles viewed as "a public act to indemnify murder"[5]), and the disillusionment of the mission to Native Americans intensified the passion of the brothers for the outcasts of society. Finally, this description (probably written by Sarah Wesley) of the social task and engagement of Charles and John is both succinct and insightful:

They were neither to be intimidated by danger, affected by interest, or deterred by disgrace: and surely it required no common degree of resolution to expose themselves to the rude ignorance of the best censure of their particular friends; yet all these evils were incurred by this mode of reforming the outcasts of mankind. It is not possible to imagine that, in their situation in life, men of learning and abilities, distinguished by academic honours, could have been actuated by any motive but the purest benevolence.[6]

The labouring poor are the most numerous class in every country; they are not less necessary to the happiness of a nation than to the higher ranks of society. In the year 1738 their education

148

was totally neglected; few of them were taught the duty of attending churches, and there was no possibility of doing them good but by some extraordinary mode of communication, as their ignorance and vicious habits removed them out of the reach of those salutary methods appointed by government.

It was a matter of national importance that so large a part of the community should be instructed in the principles of religion and the social duties of life; and it is in this point that the names of John and Charles Wesley and the Rev. George Whitefield will be peculiarly held in honour by the candid and unprejudiced.

They directed their labours to those who had no instructor, to the highways and hedges; to the miners in Cornwall and Newcastle, and the colliers in Bristol. These unhappy creatures married and buried among themselves, and often committed murders with impunity. It was always dangerous to pass their woods till these clergymen visited them, and, by their active and unremitting endeavours, a sense of morals, decency, and religion, was introduced: the ignorant were instructed, the wretched relieved, and the abandoned reclaimed. In their arduous task they not only met with opposition from the clergy, but shameful treatment from the magistrates, who (to the disgrace of the times be it mentioned), so far from punishing or restraining a lawless mob assembled to abuse them, encouraged and often instigated their excesses.[7]

Charles Wesley's *Journal* includes records of his encounters with the poor. Here one finds him with and among the poor as friend, teacher, and pastor. The following entry in particular indicates attitudes that are formative in Charles's understanding of and ministry to the poor.

> *Thurs., June 22d [1738].* I comforted Hetty,[8] under much divine destiny because, she was not in all points affected like other believers, especially the poor; who have generally a much larger degree of confidence than the rich and learned. I have proof of this today at Mr. Searl's, where, meeting a poor woman, and convincing her of unbelief, I used a prayer for her, that God who hath chosen the poor of this world to be rich in faith, would now impart to her his unspeakable gift.[9]

That the poor's capacity for confidence includes the divine destiny of richness of faith is primary to a theology of mission, as Charles understood, interpreted, and practiced it. God is not a substitute for their need nor the "only way out" of destitution. Those who have been dispossessed by and in this world can see God more clearly than others, for nothing material stands between them and God. There-

149

fore, as Charles prays the prayer "For a Family in Want," he does not pray condescendingly for a family on the margin of society, but for a family that is sustained by the Living Bread in ways of which others can only dream. Such a family knows what it means, in the words of Charles Albert Tindley, to have "nothing between my soul and my Savior." Hence God is "the portion of the poor," for those who possess nothing, understand as no one else what it means to depend fully on God's Word.

> O God, who knowest the things we need,
>   Before thy children cry,
> Give us this day our daily bread,
>   As manna from the sky.
>
> By providential love bestowed
>   Thy blessings we receive,
> And satisfied with scanty food
>   Miraculously live.
>
> We live, but not by bread alone,
>   Without distracting care,
> A life invisible, unknown,
>   A life of faith and prayer.
>
> We on thy only word depend,
>   Who nothing here possess,
> Relieved by the unfailing Friend
>   Of indigent distress.
>
> The portion of the poor thou art,
>   Who thy commands obey,
> And trust thou never wilt depart,
>   But keep us to that day.
>
> The poor in every age and place
>   Thou dost, O God, approve
> To mark with thy distinguished grace,
>   To enrich with faith and love.[10]

A second entry from the *Journal* that informs our subject is that of Saturday, August 10th [1745]:

> I preached at Shepton-Mallet, where a great door is opening, and there are many adversaries. One of the devil's drunken champions attempted to disturb us; but my voice prevailed.
> They desired me to meet their little Society at an unusual place, to disappoint the mob. I walked forward toward the town, then

turned back over the field, to drop the people, and, springing up a rising ground, sprained or broke my leg, I knew not which; but I fell down when I offered to set my foot to the ground. The brethren carried me to an hut, which was quickly filled with the poor people. It was soon noised about town that I had broke my leg; some said my neck, and that it was a judgment upon me. The principal man of the place, Mr. P., sent me a kind message, and his bath-chair to bring me to his house. I thanked him, but declined his offer, on account of my pain, which unfitted me for any company, except that of my best friends,—the poor. With these I continued praying, singing, and rejoicing for two hours. Their love quite delighted me. Happiest they that could come near to do anything for me. When my strength was exhausted, they laid me on their bed, the best they had; but I could not sleep for pain.[11]

The poor as "his best friends" is a theme that surfaces a number of times in Charles's hymns and poems. It is a perspective that shapes his missional engagement as a clergyman and Christian. It is not enough merely to do something for the outcasts of society. They must become one's best friends! Hence, in his *Short Hymns on Select Passages of the Holy Scriptures* (1762), he wrote,

> Help me to make the poor my friends,
>   By that which paves the way to hell,
> That when our loving labour ends,
>   And dying from this earth we fail,
> Our friends may greet us in the skies
> Born to a life that never dies.[12]

Here Charles is reflecting on Luke 16:9, "Make to yourselves friends of the mammon of unrighteousness; that when ye fail, they may receive you into everlasting life."

Charles is driven by a fundamental principle which he records in his *Journal* on Thurs., July 25th [1754, at Lakenham]:

> The rain drove me into brother Edward's. Only the sincere and serious attended. The poor have a right to the Gospel. I therefore preached Christ crucified to them, from Zech. xii.10.[13]

In one of the sacred hymns/poems written "After Preaching to the Newcastle Colliers" (Hymn 2) and published in *Hymns and Sacred Poems* of 1749, Charles affirms the fulfillment of that right in his own ministry.

> Even now, All-loving Lord,
> Thou hast sent forth thy word,
>   Thou the door hast opened wide:
>   (Who can shut thy open door!)
>   I the grace have testified,
> Preached Thy Gospel to the poor.[14]

One instance in the *Journal* provides a different picture of the socially engaged Charles Wesley. Here he assumes the role of a civil arbitrator on behalf of the poor. The entry for July 5th [1751] describes an incident at Worcester at which rioters were present and he doubted whether he had any business there at the time. "Yet," he says, "at the desire of the poor people, I went to their room at seven."[15] Thereafter, the rioters began creating havoc by throwing dust on everyone. Charles immediately went to the Mayor.

> I spent an hour with him, pleading the poor people's cause. He said he had never before heard of their being so treated; that is, pelted, beat, and wounded, their house battered, and windows, partitions, locks broke; that none had applied to him for justice, or he should have granted it; that he was well assured of the great mischief the Methodists had done throughout the nation, and the great riches Mr. Whitefield and their other teachers had acquired; that their societies were quite unnecessary, since the Church was sufficient; that he was for having neither Methodist nor Dissenter.
> I easily answered his objections. He treated me with civility and freedom, and promised, at parting, to do our people justice. Whether he does or not, I have satisfied my own conscience.[16]

This view of Charles as the civil arbitrator recalls the Charles Wesley in Georgia negotiating a settlement with a Native American tribe. As Tories and supporters of the monarchy, Charles and John Wesley were not engaged in efforts to reform the governmental and societal structures which perpetuated oppression of the poor in the eighteenth-century England, but they did attack head-on the problems and results of such oppression within English society. The account just cited clearly shows that civil disobedience often evoked significant exercise of civil responsibility, even from Charles, to the extent that a civil authority was confronted with injustice against the poor.

Remembering the Social Imperatives of the Gospel

For Charles Wesley, as for John, the gospel places social imperatives at the heart of the Christian life. This is stated clearly in their
preface to *Hymns and Sacred Poems* (1742):

> First, *we not only allow, but* earnestly contend, (as for the Faith once
> delivered to the Saints) *That there is no Perfection in this Life which
> implies any Differentiation from attending All the Ordinances of GOD, or
> from* doing Good unto All Men, while we have Time, *tho'* 'specially
> unto the Household of Faith.[17]

Charles and John became convinced through a variety of influences, including Moravian hymn singing, that the wedding of theological verse with music provided one of the most effective ways of
celebrating and remembering faith, responsibility, and practice.
While John was the primary editor of such verse (though Frank
Baker's recent work on Charles's *Hymns for the Nativity of our Lord*
[1745][18] provides new insight on the work of Charles as an editor), it
is Charles in large measure who provides the vehicles of memory
through his own creative poetic genius.

Therefore, in the light of the citation from the Preface of *Hymns
and Sacred Poems* of 1742, it is not surprising to find what one might
perhaps call a "Wesleyan Social Manifesto" in that volume:

> Help us to help each other, Lord,
>   Each other's cross to bear,
> Let all their friendly aid afford,
>   And feel each other's care.
>
> Help us to build each other up,
>   Our little stock improve,
> Increase our Faith, confirm our Hope,
>   And perfect us in Love.[19]

Feeling the care of one's kindred is essential to faith of head and heart.
Just as one must *feel* the blood of Christ applied, so must one *feel* the
care of others.[20]

The Language of the Poor

Charles Wesley prompts the church's memory of the social imperatives of the gospel and particularly its engagement with the poor
by using language that has its social location among the poor and
outcast. He uses metaphors, similes, figures of speech, and nomen-

clature with which the dispossessed of eighteenth-century English society could identify.

The poverty stricken, who received little or no medical care for ailments or physical impairments, heard an unfamiliar invitation (to the Great Supper) in the words:

> Come, all ye souls by sin oppressed,
> Ye restless wanderers after rest;
> Ye poor, and maimed, and halt, and blind,
> In Christ a hearty welcome find.[21]

The prisons of the day were filled with persons arrested for debts, who had been entrapped by insidious laws and become victims of grave injustices. No doubt they identified with the following words in ways others could not:

> Poor debtors by our Lord's request,
> A full acquittance we receive;
> And criminals, with pardon blest,
> We at our Judge's instance live.[22]

Notice the language: debtors, acquittance, criminals, pardon, judge. Charles packs into four lines words that are integral to the daily fate of innumerable prisoners of eighteenth-century England and transforms them into words of hope. What welcome thoughts for prisoners, who often had to bribe their guards with money just to have their chains taken off for a few hours during the day, were Wesley's lines:

> My chains fell off, my heart was free,
> I rose, went forth, and followed thee.[23]

From Charles the dispossessed of society hear what they do not hear in the workplace, the street, courts, or prisons: they are on an equal level in this world with every other human being before God. They too are called and loved by God. The unloved are loved.

> Love immense and unconfined,
> Love to all of humankind,
> Love, which willeth all should live,
> Love, which all to all would give,
> Love, that over all prevails,
> Love, that never, never fails:
> Stand secure, for thou shalt prove
> All the eternity of love.[24]

Charles's summons to the dispossessed is expressed much more explicitly in the following lines:

> Outcasts of men, to you I call,
> Harlots, and publicans, and thieves!
> He spreads his arms to embrace you all,
> Sinners alone his grace receives:
> No need of him the righteous have;
> He came the lost to seek and save![25]

> He hath opened a door
> To the penitent poor,
> And rescued from sin,
> And admitted the harlots and publicans in.
> They have heard the glad sound,
> They have liberty found
> Through the blood of the Lamb,
> And plentiful pardon in Jesus's name.[26]

Hymns for Ministry to the Poor

Charles Wesley creates a hymnic, poetically remembered theology that articulates the imperatives of ministry to the poor.

(1) God's universal love includes the poor. God has chosen them and marked them as recipients of God's grace and for the enrichment of faith and love. In reflecting on Luke 4:26, "Unto none of them was Elias sent, save unto a woman that was a widow," Wesley wrote:

> The poor I to the rich prefer,
> If with thine eyes I see,
> To bear thy Spirit's character
> The poor are chose by Thee:
> The poor in every age and place
> Thou dost, O God, approve
> To mark with thy distinguished grace,
> To enrich with faith and love.[27]

The inclusivity of God's love is affirmed for him also in Matthew 2:10: "So those servants went out into the highways, and gathered together all as many as they found, both bad and good: and the wedding was furnished with guests."

> God his grace on them bestows
> Whom he vouchsafes to call,
> No respect of persons knows,
> But offers Christ to all:

> In the wedding-garment clad
> (The faith which God will not reprove)
> Poor and rich, and good and bad
> May banquet on his love.[28]

(2) The poor vicariously occupy Christ's place in the world; hence, faithful response to them is faithful response to Christ. Wesley understands Matthew 26:11, "Ye have the poor always with you," in this manner:

> Yes, the poor supply thy place,
>   Still deputed, Lord, by thee,
> Daily exercise our grace,
>   Prove our growing charity;
> What to them with right intent
>   Truly, faithfully is given,
> We have to our Saviour lent,
>   Laid up for ourselves in heaven.[29]

The constancy of the poor's presence should evoke a conscious daily exercise of mercy as evidence of unending growth in charity and love throughout one's life. What one offers to the poor, one offers to Christ. This is not an abstract theological concept for Charles, but a living reality.

(3) Love and care of the poor are primary for followers of Christ. They are the highest of callings.

> The poor as Jesus' bosom-friends,
>   The poor he makes his latest care,
> To all his successors commends,
>   And wills us on our hands to bear:
> The poor our dearest care we make,
>   Aspiring to superior bliss,
> And cherish for their Saviour's sake,
>   And love them with a love like his.[30]

Christ's intimate friends are the poor! For Charles it is taken for granted that one cannot be a friend of Christ without being a friend of the poor. Furthermore, love of the poor is not simply a "beautiful idea" commended by Christ to his followers; rather it is the will of Christ to be borne on one's hands, with which one is to touch, heal, comfort, and care for the poor. Such care is, Charles says, "superior bliss."

(4) The poor bring Christian perspectives on wealth and riches into proper focus. It is clear that John Wesley, while discouraging confidence in worldly wealth, encouraged members of the societies to be economically productive and to use their resources of gain for the good of the gospel and care of the weak. He does not call for a dispossession of all wealth, however.[31] Charles largely shares John's view here, but borders on calling for total dispossession of all earthly gain. Of Acts 20:33, "I coveted no one's silver or gold or clothing," Charles says:

> The servant of a Master poor,
> Possest of treasures that endure,
> Can no terrestrial good desire,
> Silver, or gold, or gay attire;
> Nor will he judge who riches have,
> Limit the Almighty's power to save,
> Or lump them with invidious zeal,
> And rashly send them all to hell.[32]

Charles's letters to his wife indicate, however, that, as did John, he sought to practice a responsible personal financial policy and hence did not totally renounce all earthly goods in an ascetic sense. Yet he struggled greatly with the question of wealth and possessions. This is nowhere more evident than in his powerful and heart-rending response to Acts 4:34-5, "There was not a needy person among them, for as many as owned lands or houses sold them and brought the proceeds of what was sold. They laid it at the apostles' feet, and it was distributed to each as any had need."

> Which of the Christians now
>   Would his possessions sell?
> The fact ye scarce allow,
>   The truth incredible,
> That men of old so weak should prove,
> And as themselves their neighbour love.
>
> Of your redundant store
>   Ye may a few relieve,
> But all to feed the poor
>   Ye cannot, cannot give,
> Houses or lands for Christ forego,
> Or live as Jesus lived below.

157

Jesus, thy church inspire
    With Apostolic love,
Infuse the one desire
    T'insure our wealth above,
Freely with earthly goods to part,
And joyfully sell all in heart.

With thy pure Spirit filled,
    And loving Thee alone,
We shall our substance yield,
    Call nothing here our own,
Whate'er we have or are submit
And lie, as beggars, at thy feet.[33]

The desire "Freely with earthly goods to part" is at the heart of Wesley's social task, for one's resources are to be used for the salvation, care, comfort, well-being, and improvement of others. Followers of Christ are to "call nothing here our own" (stanza 4, line 4).

(5) The sacraments of the church belong to the poor. The Lord's table knows no exclusivity:

Come, sinners, to the gospel feast;
Let every soul be Jesu's guest;
Ye need not one be left behind,
For God hath bidden all mankind.

.   .   .   .

Come, all ye souls by sin oppressed,
Ye restless wanderers after rest;
Ye poor, and maimed, and halt, and blind,
In Christ a hearty welcome find.[34]

We learn from Charles's *Journal* that he administered Holy Communion to felons, indigents, colliers, and simply the poor. His pastoral concern thrust him into the prisons of Newgate, Oxford, and elsewhere to preach, counsel, read prayers, comfort the condemned, assist with physical needs, and share the body and blood of Christ. He ministered to white and black alike, to thief and murderer.

(6) The ministerial office embodies a mandate of service to the poor. Charles wrote numerous poems that describe and evaluate the office of ministry. In a hymn based on Acts 4:36-7, he draws an analogy for the office from the action of Barnabas, a Levite who sold a field and brought the money and laid it at the apostles' feet.

158

Ye Levites hired who undertake
    The aweful ministry
For lucre or ambition's sake,
    A nobler pattern see!
Who greedily your pay receive,
    And adding cure to cure,
In splendid ease and pleasures live
    By pillaging the poor.

See here an apostolic priest,
    Commissioned from the sky,
Who dares of all vain self divest,
    The needy to supply!
A primitive example rare
    Of gospel-poverty,
To feed the flock one's only care,
    And like the Lord to be.

Jesus, to us apostles raise,
    Like-minded pastors give
Who freely may dispense thy grace
    As freely they receive;
Who disengaged from all below
    May earthly things despise,
And every creature-good forego
    For treasure in the skies.[35]

"Priests" faithful to the apostolic office are willing to follow Barnabas' example and divest themselves of "all" in order to supply the needy!

Charles knew the dangers of wealth to the office of ministry. On one occasion in MS Preachers (1786), he spoke of clergy who, when they began, had hearts that were rightly disposed and only lived to serve God, but they have been corrupted by money, food, and clothing. At first their only hope and aim was Jesus, but the love of earthly things has corrupted them.

Genteelity we now affect,
    Fond to adorn the outward man,
Nice in our dress, we court respect
    And female admiration gain;
As men of elegance and taste
    We slight, and overlook the poor,
But in the rich, with servile haste
    Contend to make our interest sure.[36]

He accentuates the clergy's divesting itself of responsibility to the poor even more strongly in the following critique, also found in MS Preachers:

> The weak, the simple, and the poor
> Within thy mercy's arms secure
>   With confidence we leave:
> But O the strong, the rich, the wise,
> Ee'r their last spark of goodness dies
>   Revisit and forgive.[37]

Charles personalizes these perspectives in a poem written in the first person in the same manuscript, a prayer for a life of poverty and toil in service to Christ.

> While preaching gospel to the poor,
> My soul impoverish, and secure
>   By deep humility;
> Safe in thy wounds a novice hide,
> Then shall I preach the Crucified,
>   And nothing know but thee.
>
> Here may I covet no reward,
> Nor triffles temporal regard,
>   Or reckon earth my home,
> But things invisible desire,
> And wait for my appointed hire
>   Till the great Shepherd come.
>
> A life of poverty and toil,
> A thousand lives, one gracious smile
>   Of thine will overpay,
> If thou receive me with well done,
> And for thy faithful servant own,
>   In that triumphant day.[38]

(7) Discipleship to Christ means social engagement on behalf of the poor and dispossessed. All of the above imperatives are the foundation for Charles's equation of discipleship and social duty/action. While his hymns and poems do utilize language with which the outcasts of society could identify, and many of his hymns remind the church of its responsibilities to them, almost no current hymnals contain hymns by Wesley that challenge the church to specific tasks of social activity for the poor and dispossessed. Yet he did articulate

for the church's memory the social imperatives of discipleship, which are expressed in the following hymn never included in a hymnal:

Your duty let the Apostle show:
Ye ought, ye ought to labour so,
    In Jesus' cause employed,
Your calling's works at times pursue,
And keep the tent-maker in view,
    And use your hands for God.

Work for the weak, and sick, and poor,
Raiment and food for them procure,
    And mindful of his word,
Enjoy the blessedness to give,
Lay out your gettings, to relieve
    The members of your Lord.

Your labour which proceeds from love,
Jesus shall graciously approve,
    With full felicity,
With brightest crowns your loan repay,
And tell you in that joyful day
    "Ye did it unto Me."[39]

The support of the weak is a duty of discipleship, not an option, and involves manual labor, the use of one's hands. It is Jesus' cause and has been exemplified in the apostle Paul. Charles spells out the social task for Christ's disciples. They are to: (1) work for the weak, sick and poor; (2) procure food and clothing for them; and (3) give of their financial resources in order to provide them relief. The motivation for such action issues from one source—love!

Such statements by Charles Wesley are not numerous in his hymnody, but it is clear that he by no means ignored the social task of discipleship and how it should be implemented.

In Praise of the Saints' Ministry to the Poor

In many of his poems written on the occasion of someone's death, Charles Wesley identified models of Christian discipleship, exemplary behavior that demonstrates the implementation of the social imperatives of the gospel. In verse he praises certain individuals who have been faithful stewards of their lives and resources as followers of Jesus Christ.

161

Mrs. Mary Naylor, who died on March 21, 1757, is described by Charles Wesley as a person whose every thought was controlled by justice. Above all, she was a nursing-mother to the poor. She exemplified total commitment to the poor. Her entire existence was consumed with labor for the poor. Such actualization of good is godlike. Here one finds a classic Wesleyan paradigm of the wedding of head, heart, and hands: the central focus of her thoughts is justice, her soul was moved by affliction, poverty, and distress, and she labored endlessly on behalf of the poor.

> The golden rule she has pursued,
> And did to others as she would
> Others should do to her;
> Justice composed her upright soul,
> Justice did all her thoughts control,
> And formed her character.
>
> Affliction, poverty, disease,
> Drew out her soul in soft distress,
> The wretched to relieve:
> In all the works of love employed,
> Her sympathizing soul enjoyed
> The blessedness to give.
>
> Her Savior in his members seen,
> A stranger she received him in,
> An hungry Jesus fed,
> Tended her sick, imprisoned Lord,
> And flew in all his wants to afford
> Her ministerial aid.
>
> A nursing-mother to the poor,
> For them she husbanded her store,
> Her life, her all, bestowed;
> For them she labored day and night,
> In doing good her whole delight,
> In copying after God.
>
> Away, my tears and selfish sighs!
> The happy saint in paradise
> Requires us not to mourn;
> But rather keep her life in view,
> And still her shining steps pursue,
> Till all to God return.[40]

Mrs. Elizabeth Blackwell, who died on March 27, 1772, is also one who is singled out by Wesley for "Nursing the poor with constant care." Wherever she found the sick and the poor, she was willing to spend her life for them. She possessed an empathy through which a sufferer's despair became her own. Such a person is one who confesses God in all her ways. Faithful discipleship to the Savior reveals living faith by works. This is the personification of the social imperatives of the gospel:

> Touching the legal righteousness,
>   While blameless in thy sight she lived,
> Thee she confessed in all her ways,
>   And all her good from thee received;
> Faithful even then, she flew to tend,
>   Where'er distressed, the sick and poor,
> Rejoiced for them her life to spend,
>   And all thy gifts through them restore.
>
> Her living faith by works was shown:
>   Through faith to full salvation kept,
> She made the sufferer's griefs her own,
>   And wept sincere with those that wept:
> Nursing the poor with constant care,
>   Affection soft, and heart-esteem,
> She saw her Saviour's image there,
>   And gladly ministered to him.[41]

In the following verse, "On the Death of Mr. Thomas Lewis," who died in April of 1782, Wesley stresses yet another model of discipleship, that of sacrificial service. Mr. Lewis's self-denial is a deprivation for the sake of others, namely, the sick and poor. He has given up his own food that the hungry might be fed.

> A father to the sick and poor,
> For them he husbanded his store,
>   For them himself denied;
> The naked clothed, the hungry fed
> Or parted with his daily bread
>   That they might be supplied.[42]

Mr. Ebenezer Blackwell, who died on April 21, 1782, embodied yet another model of discipleship that fulfills the social imperatives of the gospel for Wesley, namely, a financial or economic one. His life demonstrated the responsible use of resources for the poor:

163

> Afflictions kind, unfailing friend,
>   He wisely used his growing store,
> And prized his privilege to lend
>   To God—by giving to the poor.
> The Lord his liberal servant blessed,
>   Who paid him back the blessing given;
> And still, the more his wealth increased,
>   More treasure he laid up in heaven.[43]

The above persons fulfill the hope that Charles Wesley expressed for all Christians in the conclusion of his sermon "Faith and Works," which was first preached in December 21, 1738:

> You should see and revere your Saviour in every poor man you ease, and be as ready to relieve him as you would to relieve Christ Himself. Is Christ an hungered? Give Him meat. Is He thirsty? Give Him drink. Is He a stranger? Take ye Him in. Clothe Him when He is naked; visit Him when He is sick. When He is in prison, come ye unto Him.[44]

The Impact of Charles Wesley's Message of Ministry with the Poor

What conclusions can be drawn regarding the impact of Charles Wesley's message on socially engaged discipleship and ministry with the poor? It must be noted that numerous texts quoted above were never published and hence until now have had no general impact at all. Certainly Wesley hymns are not known as "social action" hymns. The selections of his texts in most hymnals reflect strong doctrinal statements often embedded in an intense inner spiritual journey and in evangelical/sacramental theology.

The Wesley hymns that survive in hymnals also tend to reflect a "spiritualized" concept of "the poor." This is not surprising, since Charles himself spiritualized it in many verses. The well-known summons to the dispossessed of society in Charles's conversion hymn is generally perceived in a spiritualized sense:

> Outcasts of men, to you I call,
>   Harlots and publicans, and thieves!
> He spreads his arms to embrace you all,
>   Sinners alone his grace receives:
> No need of him the righteous have;
> He came the lost to seek and save![45]

This is heard and sung as a call to redemption and salvation of the outcasts of society, but not as a call to their socialization. It has traditionally been much easier for the church to invite the poor to salvation, for Christ died for them too, than to invite them to their rightful place in society as children of God, i.e., to socialization—to become friends, brothers, sisters, kindred in the faith and in the church, persons with whom one daily shares and walks, and whom one comforts. The message that Christ embraces all the dispossessed of the earth has been preached with fervor, but the church itself and its members often have not done as Christ did and truly *embraced* them all.

Part of the problem lies in the fact that we are divorced from the eighteenth-century social location of Wesley's language and we can understand it spiritually even if we do not understand its societal context. Nevertheless, it is very clear that Wesley himself fostered a spiritualized concept of the poor in many of his hymns and poems. His verse on Luke 14:21 ("bring in the poor, the crippled, the blind, and the lame") makes this evident.

> Needy, impotent to good,
>   Disabled, halt, and blind,
> Hungring after heavenly food
>   Our souls may mercy find:
> Sinners poor invited are
> To what the rich and full despise,
> Feasted here on Christ, they share
> His banquet in the skies.[46]

But Wesley did not leave the poor merely to the realm of the spirit. Redemption and holiness apply to the social realm as well as in his theology.

It is important to realize, however, that becoming "poor in spirit" is vital for Charles Wesley. Self-understanding of one's own poverty is the fulcrum of humility and service. This is why Jesus' words, "if the salt has lost its taste, how can its saltiness be restored?" (Luke 14:34), move him to say:

> O may I ever be
>   The least in my own eyes,
> Retain my poverty,
>   And labour for the prize,
> And always dread the apostate's doom
> And watch, and pray, till Jesus come![47]

165

In his *Short Hymns* (1762), Charles relates the concept of personal poverty to perfection. He responds to the admonition "Be ye perfect" [Greek: "Ye shall be perfect"], as follows:

> *"Ye shall be perfect"* here below,
> He spake it, and it must be so;
>   But first he said, "Be poor;
> "Hunger, and thirst, repent, and grieve,
> "In humble, meek obedience live,
>   "And labour, and endure."[48]

Wesley views personal poverty as a prerequisite to perfection. He continues:

> Thus, thus may I the prize pursue,
> And all th'appointed paths pass through
>   To perfect poverty,
> Thus let me, Lord, thyself attain,
> And give thee up thine own again,
>   Forever lost in thee.[49]

Interestingly, Christian perfection, a subject on which Charles and John by no means always agreed, is equated with perfect poverty. This is the highest level of spiritualization of the idea of the poor (poverty) to which Wesley soars. Self-effacement and divestment in one's life of everything that obstructs the personification of perfect love in every thought, word, and deed is the demand of the gospel.

> Away this soft, luxurious pride!
> A pilgrim rather let me rove,
> Poor with the Son of man abide,
> And have no comfort, but his love![50]

Yet who desires such poverty? he asks. "Foxes have holes, and birds of the air have nests; but the Son of Man has nowhere to lay his head" (Luke 9:58):

> Saviour, how few there are
> Who thy condition share,
> Few who cordially embrace,
>   Love, and prize thy poverty,
> Want on earth a resting-place,
>   Needy and resigned like Thee![51]

Perhaps Charles's innovative concept of "perfect poverty" would do more to revive the idea of Christian perfection in our time than might be imagined.

The impact of Charles Wesley's message to the poor has been rather one-sided. When one examines the editorial selection of his hymns in hymnals, it is evident that this process has generally favored a spiritualized concept of the poor. However, Wesley perceives the demand of the gospel not only to call the poor and dispossessed to salvation but to make them our "best friends"— evangelization and socialization.

John Wesley included in the 1780 *A Collection of Hymns for the Use of The People Called Methodists* Charles's hymn "Try us, O God, and search the Ground," which appeared in a number of succeeding hymnals in the Methodist tradition. It contains two stanzas that address the Christian's social engagement. They are quoted above on page 5, beginning with the line, "Help us to help each other, Lord."

The church's memory of Charles Wesley's message to the poor is minuscule at best and a contemporary appropriation of the Wesleyan heritage will be greatly strengthened by a recovery, at least in the hymnic memory of the church, of his texts that wed evangelization and socialization of the poor. This places firmly in the theological memory of the church the paradigm of faith that integrates head, heart, and hands.

In conclusion, I quote one surviving stanza among the Wesley hymns of British Methodism's *Hymns and Psalms* (1983). It is one of the few remaining stanzas of Charles Wesley's in any contemporary hymnal that sustains this memory: stanza 4 of "Jesus, the gift divine I know" (No. 318):

> Thy mind throughout my life be shown,
>   While listening to the sufferer's cry,
> The widow's and the orphan's groan,
>   On mercy's wings I swiftly fly,
> The poor and helpless to relieve,
> My life, my all, for them to give.

Contributors

Victorio Araya-Guillén is Professor of Theology at the Seminario Bíblico Latinoamericano, San José, Costa Rica and at the Ecumenical School of Religious Sciences at the National University of Costa Rica. He has a Licenciatura in Theology from the Seminario Bíblico Latinamericano, a Masters in Philosophy from the University of Costa Rica, and a Doctorate in Theology from the Pontifical University of Salamanca. He is the author of *Fe cristiana y Marxismo: Una perspectiva en A.L.* (Ed. Territorio), *Lectura Política de la Biblia* (Sebila), and *God of the Poor* (Orbis Books).

Rebecca S. Chopp is Professor of Systematic Theology and Dean of the Faculty and Academic Affairs at Candler School of Theology, Emory University, Atlanta, Georgia. She studied at Kansas Wesleyan and has the M.Div. degree from Saint Paul School of Theology and the Ph.D. from The University of Chicago Divinity School. Her publications include *The Praxis of Suffering: An Interpretaion ot Liberation and Political Theologies* (Orbis Books) and *The Power to Speak: Feminism, Language and God* (Crossroad), and (with Duane F. Parker) *Liberation Theology and Pastoral Theology* (JPC Publications).

Donald W. Dayton is Professor of Theology and Ethics at Northern Baptist Theological Seminary in Lombard, Illinois. He holds degrees from Houghton College (B.A.), Yale University Divinity School (B.D.), the University of Kentucky (M.S.), and the University of Chicago (Ph.D.). He is author of *Discovering an Evangelical Heritage* (Harper & Row), *Theological Roots of Pentecostalism* (Francis Asbury Press), and *The Variety of American Evangelicalism* (University of Tennessee Press). He is the editor of "The Higher Christian Life," a 48-volume series of facsimile reprints for the study of the holiness movement and pentecostalism.

Richard P. Heitzenrater is Professor of Church History and Wesley Studies at The Divinity School of Duke University in Durham, North Carolina. He received the B.A., the M.Div., and Ph.D. degrees from Duke University. His publications include *The Elusive Mr. Wesley*, 2 vols. (Abingdon Press), *Diary of an Oxford Methodist: Benjamin Ingham, 1733–1734* (Duke University Press), *Mirror and Memory: Reflections on Early Methodism* (Kingswood Books), and *Wesley and the People Called Methodists* (Abingdon Press). He is General Editor of the Wesley Works Editorial Project which is producing the thirty-five volume *Bicentennial Edition of the Works of John Wesley* (Abingdon Press) and, with W. Reginald Ward, editor of several volumes of Wesley's *Journal and Diaries* in that series.

Theodore W. Jennings, Jr. is Professor of Constructive Theology at Chicago Theological Seminary. He holds degrees from Duke University (B.A.), Candler School of Theology, Emory University (B.D.), and Emory University (Ph.D.). His publications include *Beyond Theism: A Grammar of God-Language* (Oxford University Press), *Good News to the Poor: John Wesley's Evangelical Economics* (Abingdon Press), and *Loyalty to God: The Apostles Creed in Life and Liturgy* (Abingdon Press).

S T Kimbrough, Jr. is Executive Secretary of Mission Evangelism for the General Board of Global Ministries of The United Methodist Church. He is graduate of Birmingham Southern College (B.A.) and the Divinity School of Duke University (M.Div.) and holds a P.D. in Old Testament and Semitic Languages from Princeton Theological Seminary. He has published *Israelite Religion in Sociological Perspective* (Harrassowitz), and is the editor of *A Song for the Poor: Hymns by Charles Wesley* (The Mission Education and Cultivation Program Department of the General Board of Global Ministries, The United Methodist Church), *Charles Wesley: Poet and Theologian* (Kingswood Books), and (with Oliver A. Beckerlegge) *The Unpublished Poetry of Charles Wesley*, 3 vols. (Kingswood Books).

M. Douglas Meeks is Professor of Systematic Theology and Academic Dean at Wesley Theological Seminary in Washington, D.C. His undergraduate degree is from Rhodes College. He received the B.D. from Duke Divinity School and the Ph.D. from Duke University with graduate work at Tübingen University, Germany. His publications include *Origins of the Theology of Hope* (Fortress Press), and *God the Economist: The Doctrine of God and Political Economy* (Fortress Press).

He has previously edited the volumes eminating from the Oxford Instiute of Methodist Theological Studies in 1982 and 1987: *The Future of Methodist Theological Traditions* (Abingdon Press) and *What Should Methodists Teach? Wesleyan Traditions and Modern Diversity* (Kingswood Books).

Itumeleng Mosala is Professor of Old Testament at The University of Cape Town, South Africa. He received the M.A. degree from Manchester University and the Ph.D. from The University of Cape Town. He is author of *The Unquestionable Right to Be Free* (Orbis Books), *Hammering Swords into Ploughshares* (Skotaville, Johannesburg), and *Biblical Hermeneutics and Black Theology* (Wm. B. Eerdmans).

David Lowes Watson is Professor of Theology and Congregational Life and Mission at Wesley Theological Seminary in Washington, D.C. He was educated at Oxford University (M.A.), Eden Theological Seminary (M.Div.), and Duke University (Ph.D.). He has published *Accountable Discipleship, The Early Methodist Class Meeting*, and *Class Leaders: Recovering a Tradition* (all Discipleship Resources), and *God Does Not Foreclose: The Universal Promise of Salvation* (Abingdon Press).

Abbreviations

Journal   *The Journal of the Rev. John Wesley, A.M.*, ed. Nehemiah Curnock, 8 vols. (London: Epworth Press, 1909–16).

Journal CW   *The Journal of the Rev. Charles Wesley, M.A.*, ed. Thomas Jackson, 2 vols. (London: John Mason, 1849; reprinted Grand Rapids: Baker Book House, 1980).

Letters   *The Letters of the Rev. John Wesley, A.M.*, ed. John Telford, 8 vols. (London: Epworth Press, 1931).

Poetry   *The Unpublished Poetry of Charles Wesley*, ed. S T Kimbrough, Jr., and Oliver A. Beckerlegge, 3 vols. (Nashville: Kingswood Books, 1988–1992).

Sermons CW   *Sermons by the Late Rev. Charles Wesley, A.M.* (London: Baldwin, Craddock and Joy, 1816).

Works   *The Works of John Wesley;* begun as "The Oxford Edition of The Works of John Wesley" (Oxford: Clarendon Press, 1975–1983); continued as "The Bicentennial Edition of The Works of John Wesley" (Nashville: Abingdon Press, 1984—); 14 of 35 vols. published to date.

Works (J)   *The Works of John Wesley*, ed. Thomas Jackson, 14 vols. (London: Wesleyan Conference Office, 1872; reprint, Grand Rapids, MI: Zondervan, [1958–59]).

Notes

Notes to Chapter 1

1. More detailed information of Wesley's views on this matter is presented in my *Good News to the Poor: John Wesley's Evangelical Economics* (Nashville: Abingdon Press, 1990). Some of this material has also appeared in "Wesley's Preferential Option for the Poor," *Quarterly Review* 9/3 (Fall, 1989), 10–29.

2. "The Signs of the Times," *Works (J)* 8:308.

3. *A Farther Appeal to Men of Reason and Religion*, Part III, *Works (J)* 8:239.

4. *Works (J)* 2:178 (March 29, 1750).

5. *Works (J)* 1:490 (April 15, 1745).

6. *Works (J)* 3:178 (May 21, 1764).

7. John Walsh, "John Wesley and the Community of Goods," in Keith Robbins, ed., *Protestant Evangelicalism: Britain, Ireland, Germany, and America, c.1750–c.1950: Essays in Honor of W. Reginald Ward*, Studies in Church History 7 (Oxford: Basil Blackwell, 1990), 25–50.

8. "On Visiting the Sick," *Works (J)* 7:117. See also: "On Zeal," *Works (J)* 2:60.

9. *Works (J)* 7:119.

10. *Works (J)* 4:296 (Feb. 13, 1785); cf. *Works (J)* 4:358 (Feb. 8, 1787).

11. *Works (J)* 4:295 (Jan. 4, 1785).

12. "Large Minutes," *Works (J)* 8:332.

13. "Sermon on the Mount," *Works (J)* 8:377.

14. "Danger of Increasing Riches," *Works (J)* 7:362. See also "The More Excellent Way," *Works (J)* 7:36.

15. "On Dress," *Works (J)* 7:21.

16. José Míguez Bonino, "Wesley's Doctrine of Sanctification From a Liberationist Perspective," in Theodore Runyon, ed., *Sanctification and Liberation: Liberation Theologies in Light of the Wesleyan Tradition* (Nashville: Abingdon Press, 1981), 49–63.

17. This theme is pursued in Pablo Richard, et al., *The Idols of Death and the God of Life: A Theology* (Maryknoll, N.Y.: Orbis Books, 1983) and

175

Franz Hinkelammert, *The Ideological Weapons of Death*, tr. Phillip Berryman (Maryknoll, N.Y.: Orbis Books, 1986).

18. "Thoughts on the Present Scarcity of Provisions," Works (J) 11:53–59.

19. See Dow Kirkpatrick, "A Liberating Pastoral for the Rich," in Runyon, ed., *Sanctification and Liberation*, 209–23.

20. *Works (J)* 12:140 (Letter to Charles Wesley, Nov. 4, 1772).

21. See Andrew Sung Park, "Theology of Han," *Quarterly Review* (Spring, 1989), 48–62. See also Park, *The Wounded Heart of God: The Asian Concept of Han and the Christian Doctrine of Sin* (Nashville: Abingdon Press, 1993).

22. *Works (J)* 12:78–9 (Letter to Mr. John Smith, June 25, 1746).

23. I have attempted to argue for this in *Loyalty to God: The Apostles Creed in Life and Liturgy* (Nashville: Abingdon Press, 1992).

24. "The New Creation," *Works (J)* 6:288–296.

25. *Works (J)* 6:241–52.

26. In Africa, Itumeleng J. Mosala, *Biblical Hermeneutics and Black Theology in South Africa* (Grand Rapids: William B. Eerdmans, 1989), and Canaan Banana have been among those who have opened new vistas for the reading of the texts in this way; as have Elisabeth Schüssler Fiorenza, *In Memory of Her* (New York: Crossroad, 1983), and Rebecca S. Chopp, *The Power to Speak: Feminism, Language, God* (New York: Crossroad, 1991), in the United States, and José Miranda, *Marx and the Bible* (Maryknoll, N.Y.: Orbis Books, 1974), in Latin America.

27. Justo L. González, *Faith and Wealth: A History of Early Christian Ideas on the Origin, Significance, and Use of Money* (San Francisco: Harper and Row, 1990).

28. Clement of Alexandria, "Who is the Rich Man that Shall be Saved?" in *The Ante-Nicene Fathers*, American Edition, 10 vols. (New York: Scribner's, 1908–11), 2:589–604.

29. See "Why Did Wesley Fail" in my *Good News to the Poor*, 157–179.

30. See *Wesley's Standard Sermons*, ed. E. H. Sugden, 2 vols. (London: Epworth Press, 1921), 1:97–98, 493–494, where Sugden fails to indicate to the reader the significance of this for Wesley and proposes interpretations that flatly contradict Wesley's *Explanatory Notes Upon the New Testament* (q.v.).

31. Here I have in mind studies such as that of James Cochrane of the mainline churches in South Africa aptly titled *Servants of Power* (Ravan Press, 1987), or the reflections of David Kwang-sun Suh on the way in which the radical protestantism of turn-of-the-century Korea was deflected by an evangelistic campaign seeking to turn attention away from the concrete historical problems of the minjung to "spiritual" issues. See "Minjung and Theology in Korea: A Biographical Sketch of an Asian Theological Consultation" in Kim Yong Bok, ed., *Minjung Theology: People as the Subjects of History* (Christian Conference of Asia, 1981), 17–39.

32. *A Farther Appeal to Men of Reason and Religion,* Part II, *Works (J)* 8:187.

33. "The Signs of the Times," *Works (J)* 6:308.

Notes to Chapter 2

1. John D. Levenson, "Liberation Theology and the Exodus," *Midstream* (October, 1989), 30–36.

2. Renita Weems, "The Hebrew Women are Not Like the Egyptian Women: The Ideology of Race, Gender and Sexual Reproduction in Exodus 1," unpublished paper, 11.

3. John van Seters, "Reconstructing the Past: The Yahwist's Historiographic Method in Exodus," *Scandanavian Journal of the Old Testament* (1992).

4. In Theodore Runyon, ed., *Sanctification and Liberation: Liberation Theologies in Light of the Wesleyan Tradition* (Nashville: Abingdon Press, 1981), 60.

5. Ibid.

6. "The Bible: Is Interclass Reading Legitimate?" in Norman K. Gottwald, ed., *The Bible and Liberation* (Maryknoll, N.Y.: Orbis Books, 1983), 62.

7. *Tribute* (February/March, 1986), 176.

Notes to Chapter 3

1. For Wesley's own account of the Methodists' assistance in "temporal things," see "A Plain Account of the People Called Methodists" in *Works* 9:272–80. Several modern commentaries will be mentioned below.

2. Manfred Marquardt, *John Wesley's Social Ethics: Praxis and Principles* (Nashville: Abingdon Press, 1992). This is a translation by John E. Steely and W. Stephen Gunter of the original German edition, entitled *Praxis und Prinzipien der Sozialethik John Wesleys* (Göttingen: Vandenhoeck & Ruprecht, 1977).

3. *Works* 2:162–63.

4. Theodore W. Jennings, Jr., *Good News to the Poor: John Wesley's Evangelical Economics* (Nashville: Abingdon Press, 1990).

5. Ibid., 57, quoting a letter of June 9, 1775, in *Letters* 6:153.

6. Jennings artificially supports this wrong assumption by occasionally putting words in Wesley's mouth; e.g., "the poor of the society [of London]," implying the broader society rather than the Methodist society. See ibid., 59.

7. Henry Abelove, *The Evangelist of Desire: John Wesley and the Methodists* (Stanford: Stanford University Press, 1990).

8. See the chapter on "Daily Conduct" in Abelove, 96–109.

9. See "Plain Account," *Works* 9:275.

10. John Walsh, "John Wesley and the Community of Goods," in Keith Robbins, ed., *Protestant Evangelicalism: Britain, Ireland, Germany, and America, c.1750–c.1950: Essays in Honor of W. Reginald Ward*, Studies in Church History 7 (Oxford: Basil Blackwell, 1990), 25–50.

11. To provide the context of ethical theory within which I would like to examine Wesley's thoughts and actions regarding the poor, I rely upon a presentation on theological and social ethics by Frederick S. Carney to a session of the Ethics Colloquy at Perkins School of Theology in November, 1984. The following three-fold understanding of ethical theory is summarized from Carney's unpublished paper entitled "John Wesley's Theological Ethic."

12. Carney, 8–9; see also John Wesley, "An Israelite Indeed" (1785), *Works* 3:280.

13. *Works* 3:289.

14. "The Principles of a Methodist Farther Examined" (1746), *Works* 9:227.

15. *Works* 1:403.

16. See Richard P. Heitzenrater, *Mirror and Memory: Reflections on Early Methodism* (Nashville: Kingswood Books, 1989), 78–105, 117.

17. Ibid., 91.

18. Ibid., 98.

19. Ibid., 117.

20. Ibid., 156.

21. *Works* 4:359.

22. See *Works* 4:679.

23. *Works* 3:394

24. *Works* 3:412.

25. Letter of February 7, 1776; *Letters* 6:206–7.

26. "Circumcision of the Heart," *Works* 1:402.

27. *Works* 1:223–24.

28. "The Unity of the Divine Being," *Works* 4:66–67.

29. *Works* 1:219–20.

30. *Works* 1:407.

31. Heitzenrater, *Mirror and Memory*, 87.

32. See Carney, 13.

33. This is stated forcefully in his sermon, "The Scripture Way of Salvation," *Works* 2:153–69, and in the *Minutes* of 1770.

34. *Works* 26:259, 288–89.

35. See "The Scripture Way of Salvation," *Works* 2:163.

36. There are several other signal instances of continuity as well, which I will not get into here, such as the primacy of Scripture, original sin, prevenient grace, Christian perfection, extemporaneous preaching, field-preaching, interest in education, medicine, and prisons.

Notes to Chapter 4

1. See Justo L. González, *Faith and Wealth: A History of Early Christian Ideas on the Origin, Significance, and Use of Money* (San Francisco: Harper and Row, 1990), and his contribution to *Poverty and Ecclesiology: Nineteenth Century Evangelicals in the Light of Liberation,* ed. Anthony Dunnavant (Collegeville, MN: The Liturgical Press/Michael Glazier Books, 1992).

2. See my Epilogue to Dunnavant, ed., *Poverty and Ecclesiology.*

3. Karl Barth, *Against the Stream: Shorter Post-War Writings, 1946–52* (London: SCM Press, 1954), 36. This passage is in paragraph 17 of Barth's famous essay on "The Christian Community and the Civil Community."

4. Karl Barth, *Church Dogmatics,* IV/2 (Edinburgh: T & T Clark, 1958), 180. The German original was published in 1955.

5. I worked in advance with only Theodore W. Jennings, Jr., "Wesley's Preferential Option for the Poor," *Quarterly Review* 9 (1989), 16. This argument was then expanded in *Good News to the Poor: John Wesley's Evangelical Economics* (Nashville: Abingdon Press, 1990). My address, entitled "The Wesleyan Option for the Poor," has now been published in the *Wesleyan Theological Journal* 26/1 (Spring 1991), 7-22.

6. Perhaps I am influenced by the thorough-going and profoundly theological grounding of this principle in Barth (in the fundamental motifs of his Christology that lie at the heart of his trinitarian doctrine of God—especially that we know no other God than that revealed in Jesus Christ by the nature of the incarnation as a form of "divine condescension" that provides the "direction" for our own life in the church) to expect something more of that sort. But this is perhaps a significant point for the successive history of Methodism.

7. *Works (J)* 12:302 ("Letter to a Member of the Society," February 26, 1776).

8. *Works (J)* 1:185 (April 1, 1739).

9. Robert D. Hughes III, "Wesleyan Roots of Christian Socialism," *The Ecumenist* 13 (May–June, 1975), 50.

10. Bernard Semmel, *The Methodist Revolution* (New York: Basic Books, 1973), 17.

11. See Aaron C. H. Seymour, *The Life and Times of Selina, Countess of Huntingdon,* 2 vols. (1844), 1:27, as cited by Oscar Sherwin, *John Wesley: Friend of the People* (New York: Twayne Publishers, 1961), 40–1.

12. *Works (J)* 2:280 (February 9–10, 1753).

13. *Works (J)* 12:301 ("Letter to a Member of the Society," February 7, 1776).

14. *Works (J)* 12:302 ("Letter to a Member of the Society," February 26, 1776).

15. *Works (J)* 3:178 (May 21, 1764).

16. "Causes of the Inefficacy of Christianity," *Works (J)* 7:290.

17. I have become increasingly convinced that we need to give more attention to this issue in the life of Methodism than we have—and was pleased the hear from a friend that Albert Outler concurred in this judgment, citing my work, in a letter shortly before his death. I have developed this concept in a preliminary way in my essay, "Yet Another Layer of the Onion; Or, Opening the Ecumenical Door to Let the Riffraff In," *The Ecumenical Review* 40 (January, 1988), 87–110.

18. Donald F. Durnbaugh, *The Believers' Church: The History and Character of Radical Protestantism* (Scottdale, PA: Herald Press, 1985). This has become the classic interpretation of this strand of Christianity. The diagram is taken from p. 31.

19. Durnbaugh, 31.

20. Donald W. Dayton, *Theological Roots on Pentecostalism* (Metuchen, NJ: Scarecrow Press, 1987; paperback editions by Francis Asbury Press and more recently by Hendrickson Publishers), chapter two.

21. Colin Williams, *John Wesley's Theology Today* (Nashville: Abingdon Press, 1960), chapter nine and appendix.

22. Richard Allen, *The Life Experience and Gospel Labors of the Rt. Rev. Richard Allen* (Nashville: Abingdon Press, 1960), 30.

23. Daniel A. Payne, *The Semi-Centenary and the Retrospection of the African Methodist Episcopal Church* (Baltimore: Sherwood and Co., 1866; reprinted 1972 by "Books for Libraries"), 6.

24. Ibid., 8.

25. Ibid., 20.

26. Ibid., 21.

27. Ibid., 20.

28. See W. R. Ward, *Religion and Society in England 1790–1850* (New York: Schocken Books, 1973), and various writings of John Kent, especially *Jabez Bunting: The Last Wesleyan* (London: Epworth Press, 1955), and chapter four in *The Age of Disunity* (London: Epworth Press, 1966).

29. David Hempton, *Methodism and Politics in British Society, 1750–1850* (Stanford: Stanford University Press, 1984), 92.

30. Julia Stewart Werner, *The Primitive Methodist Connexion: Its Background and Early History* (Madison: The University of Wisconsin Press, 1984), 133.

31. Ibid., xi-xii.

32. John Petty, *The History of the Primitive Methodist Connexion.* I have used the new edition of James Macpherson (London: John Dickinson, 1880), 51.

33. Ibid., 575.

34. Ibid., 2.

35. John Munsey Turner, *Conflict and Reconciliation: Studies in Methodism and Ecumenism in England, 1740–1982* (London: Epworth Press, 1985), 88.

36. B. T. Roberts, "Free Churches," *The Earnest Christian* 1 (January,

1860), 6–10.

37. *The Earnest Christian* (March, 1871), 160, as cited by William Kostlevy, "A Preference for the Poor: Benjamin Titus Roberts and the Preferential Option for the Poor in the Early Free Methodist Church," in Dunnavant, ed., *Poverty and Ecclesiology*. See also my unpublished essay that circulates among Free Methodists under the title, "Reclaiming our Roots: The Social Vision of B. T. Roberts." On Roberts in general, see Clarence Howard Zahniser, *Earnest Christian: Life and Works of Benjamin Titus Roberts* (privately published, 1957).

38. I trace some of these themes in *Discovering an Evangelical Heritage* (San Francisco: Harper and Row, 1976; reprinted with a new preface, Peabody, MA: Hendrickson Publishers, 1988) chapter nine, 116–19.

39. This quotation is found on page 44 of the "Social Services Centenary Edition" of William Booth, *In Darkest England and the Way Out* (Atlanta: Salvation Army, 1984).

40. *Sacraments and the Salvation Army: Pneumatological Foundations*, Studies in Evangelicalism No. 10 (Metuchen, NJ: Scarecrow Press, 1990).

41. See *Discovering an Evangelical Heritage*, 118.

42. I have traced some of these currents in *Discovering an Evangelical Heritage*, especially chapter nine.

43. These developments are described in Timothy Lee Smith, *Called Unto Holiness* (Kansas City: Nazarene Publishing House, 1962), 110–15, and in Donald P. Brickley, *Man of the Morning: The Life and Work of Phineas F. Bresee* (Kansas City: Nazarene Publishing House, 1960), 135–164.

44. This is taken from the *Messenger* (September 12, 1901), as quoted in Harold Ivan Smith, *The Quotable Bresee* (Kansas City: Beacon Hill Press, 1983), 167.

45. I trace more of this theme in *Discovering an Evangelical Heritage*, chapter nine, especially 113–14.

46. H. Vinson Synan, *The Holiness-Pentecostal Movement in the United States* (Grand Rapids: William B. Eerdmans, 1971).

47. Various editions as cited above in note 20.

48. See the analysis of Jean B. A. Kessler, Jr., *A Study of the Older Protestant Missions and Churches in Peru and Chile* (Goes, Holland: Oosterbaan & Le Cointre, 1967), 103–5 and passim.

49. Ibid., 308.

50. David Martin, *Tongues of Fire: The Explosion of Protestantism in Latin America* (Oxford and Cambridge, MA: Basil Blackwell, 1990).

51. For an illustration of the growing minority of ecumenically minded and socially engaged Pentecostals, see the recent publication edited by Carmelo Alvarez, *Pentecostalismo y Liberación: Una Experiencia Latinoamericana* (San José: DEI, 1992). This volume, which came out of several conferences, including one that I attended in Chile, is part of the DEI "relectura" project of the various Latin American Protestant traditions that produced the volume that so many of us have found help on

the Methodist tradition.

52. See on this tradition, see Manuel Ossa, *Espiritualidad Popular y Acción Política: El Pastor Victor Mora y la Misión Nacional* (Santiago: Ediciones Rehue, 1990).

Notes to Chapter 5

1. Joseph Fitzmyer, *The Gospel According to Luke I–X*, Anchor Bible 28 (Garden City, NY: Doubleday, 1981).

2. Sharon H. Ringe, *Jesus, Liberation, and the Biblical Jubilee: Images for Ethics and Christology* (Philadelphia: Fortress Press, 1985).

3. Eduard Schweizer, *The Good News According to Luke*, tr. David E. Green (Atlanta: John Knox Press, 1984); and Luke T. Johnson, *Sharing Possessions: Mandate and Symbol of Faith* (Philadelphia: Fortress Press, 1981).

4. Theodore Runyon, ed., *Sanctification and Liberation: Liberation Theologies in Light of the Wesleyan Tradition* (Nashville: Abingdon Press, 1981); M. Douglas Meeks, ed., *The Future of Methodist Theological Traditions* (Nashville: Abingdon Press, 1985); and Theodore W. Jennings Jr., *Good News to the Poor: John Wesley's Evangelical Economics* (Nashville: Abingdon Press, 1990).

5. Albert C. Outler, *The Wesleyan Theological Heritage: Essays of Albert C. Outler* (Grand Rapids: Zondervan, 1991), 135.

6. See, for instance, John Hope Franklin, *From Slavery to Freedom: A History of Negro Americans*, 3rd edition (New York: Vintage, 1969); Gayraud Wilmore, *Black Religion and Black Radicalism*, 2nd edition (Maryknoll, NY: Orbis Books, 1983); and Albert Raboteau, *Slave Religion: The Invisible Institution in the Antebellum South* (New York: Oxford University Press, 1978).

7. Susie Stanley, "Empowered Foremothers: Wesleyan/Holiness Women Speak to Today's Christian Feminists," *Wesleyan Theological Journal* 24 (1989), 103–16.

8. For an examination of ecclesiologies in various liberation theologies see Peter C. Hodgson, *Revisioning the Church: Ecclesial Freedom in the New Paradigm* (Philadelphia: Fortress Press, 1988).

9. Rosemary Radford Ruether, *Women-Church: Theology and Practice of Feminist Liturgical Communities* (San Francisco: Harper & Row, 1985).

10. Theodore Runyon, "Introduction: Wesley and the Theologies of Liberation," in Runyon, ed., *Sanctification and Liberation*, 48.

11. José Míguez Bonino, "Wesley's Doctrine of Sanctification From a Liberationist Perspective," in Runyon, ed., *Sanctification and Liberation*, 58–59.

12. Cornel West, *The American Evasion of Philosophy: A Genealogy of Pragmatism* (Madison: The University of Wisconsin Press, 1989).

13. In pragmatism abduction is hypothetical, introducing new ideas,

as compared to induction, which determines values and deduction, which evolves the necessary consequences of a hypothesis. Charles Peirce explained this notion of abduction in the following manner "Deduction proves that something *must* be, induction shows that something *actually* is operative; abduction merely suggests that something *may be.*" Charles Sanders Peirce, *Collected Papers of Charles Sanders Peirce,* ed. Charles Hartshorne and Paul Weiss (Cambridge: Harvard University Press, 1960), 5:151–174.

14. Don Compier, "The Uses of Rhetoric For Theology" (unpublished Ph.D. dissertation, Emory University, 1992); Kenneth Burke, *A Rhetoric of Motives* (Berkeley: University of California Press, 1969); and Steve Mailloux, *Rhetorical Power* (Ithaca, NY, and London: Cornell University Press, 1987).

15. I mean by this claim that the function, nature, and aim of theology is itself transformation. Theology is not about explanation or verification of truth, regulation or governance of language or behavior, or investigation or interpretation of meaning, though all those moments may be interpreted as secondary to the nature of theology. Rather, in liberation theology and in Wesleyan theology, the very act of theology is as a theory of transformation.

16. Rebecca S. Chopp and Duane F. Parker, *Liberation Theology and Pastoral Theology* (Decatur, GA: JPC Publications, 1991).

17. Robert E. Chiles, *Theological Transition in American Methodism: 1790–1935* (Nashville: Abingdon Press, 1965; reprinted Lanham, New York, and London: The University Press of America, 1983.).

18. See, for instance, Harald Lindström, *Wesley and Sanctification: A Study in the Doctrine of Salvation* (London: The Epworth Press, 1950).

19. Gustavo Gutiérrez, *The God of Life,* tr. Matthew J. O'Connell, (Maryknoll, NY: Orbis Books, 1991), 116–117.

20. See, for instance, Chiles, *Theological Transition;* Vern A. Hannah, "Original Sin and Sanctification: A Problem for Wesleyans," *Wesleyan Theological Journal* 18/2 (Fall 1983), 47–53; Leon O. Hynson, "Original Sin as Privation," *Wesleyan Theological Journal* 22/2 (Fall 1987), 65–83; Carl O. Bangs, *Arminius: A Study in the Dutch Reformation* (Nashville: Abingdon Press, 1971); and Mildred Bangs Wynkoop, *A Theology of Love: The Dynamic of Wesleyanism* (Kansas City: Beacon Hill Press, 1972).

21. Rhetorically, I am suggesting that any discourse of sin needs different genres to arrive at the full complexity of destruction. Though I am not a historian of Wesleyanism, my hunch is that Wesley, undoubtably trained in rhetoric while at Oxford, implicitly used a variety of stylistic genres to describe sin. When later commentators attempt to read him through a Cartesian model of certainty and objectivity, his discourse on sin sounds confusing. Approached from the humanist tradition of rhetoric, however, Wesley may well be simply trying to describe persuasively the ongoing destruction of human life in a variety of ways.

22. Iris Marion Young, *Justice and the Politics of Difference* (Princeton: Princeton University Press, 1990).

23. *Works (J)* 6:231–40.

24. Pamela D. Couture, *Blessed are the Poor? Women's Poverty, Family Policy, and Practical Theology* (Nashville: Abingdon Press, 1991); and M. Douglas Meeks, *God the Economist: The Doctrine of God and Political Economy*, (Minneapolis: Fortress Press, 1989).

25. I want to utilize what is called poststructuralist theory to analyze the historical structuring of forms of life. Poststructuralism, in the best sense, allows the critic to identify that which must be transformed, not merely corrected. For a good introduction of poststructuralism and its use in feminist practice see Chris Weedon, *Feminist Practice and Poststructuralist Theory* (Oxford: Basil Blackwell, 1987). For the use of poststructuralism in theology see Rebecca S. Chopp, *The Power to Speak: Feminism, Language, and God* (New York: Crossroad, 1989).

26. Patricia Hill Collins, *Black Feminist Thought: Knowledge, Consciousness and the Politics of Empowerment* (New York: Routledge, 1991).

27. Ibid., 68.

28. Ibid., 69.

29. Ibid., 70.

30. Gutiérrez, *The God of Life*.

31. I am suggesting the need to reflect more on the popular expressions of art, poetry, literature that arise in prophetic movements and to use these as appropriate expressions of spirituality and hope.

32. Johannes Baptist Metz, *The Emergent Church: The Future of Christianity in a Postbourgeois World*, tr. Peter Mann (New York: Crossroad, 1981).

33. Young, *Justice and the Politics of Difference*, 236–256.

Notes to Chapter 6

1. See William J. Abraham, *The Logic of Evangelism* (Grand Rapids: William B. Eerdmans, 1989), 5ff.

2. Indeed, the two ecumenical observers at the Eighth Institute decided to stay with the evangelism working group throughout, rather than circulate among the other groups. In their report, Gillian Evans and Michael Jackson explained that their interest had been held by the way in which the very specificity of evangelistic studies had brought together a wide range of theological interests combined with pastoral and practical application. Gillian R. Evans and Michael Jackson, in "Report on Working Group V: Methodist Evangelism and Doctrine," by David Lowes Watson, *OxfordNotes* 2/3 (Fall, 1988), 11.

3. Petition No. HE-11093-3000-R, *Daily Christian Advocate (1992)*, Advance Edition, Vol. 2, p. 1234. The General Conference met in Louisville, Kentucky, May 5–15, 1992.

4. Justo L. González, "Voices of Compassion," *Missiology* 20/2 (April 1992), 163–173. This expanded issue of *Missiology*, guest edited by Stephen Bevans and Ana Maria Pineda, is devoted to the theme "Columbus and the New World: Evangelization or Invasion?"

5. This aspect of the doctrine of prevenient grace, imbibed by Wesley from seventeenth-century Anglicanism, is often overlooked. See John W. Packer, *The Transformation of Anglicanism 1643–1660, with Special Reference to Henry Hammond* (Manchester: Manchester University Press, 1969), 55ff. See also "On Working Out Our Own Salvation," *Works* 3:206–7.

6. George G. Hunter III, *How To Reach Secular People* (Nashville: Abingdon Press, 1992), 37.

7. M. Douglas Meeks, "Reflections and Open Tasks," in M. Douglas Meeks, ed., *What Should Methodists Teach? Wesleyan Tradition and Modern Diversity* (Nashville: Kingswood Books, 1990), 139. For a definitive theological treatment of this theme, see Meeks, *God the Economist: The Doctrine of God and Political Economy* (Minneapolis: Fortress Press, 1989).

8. See David J. Bosch, *Transforming Mission: Paradigm Shifts in Theology of Mission* (Maryknoll, NY: Orbis Books, 1991), 381ff., 397ff. See also Orlando E. Costas, *Christ Outside the Gate: Mission Beyond Christendom* (Maryknoll, NY: Orbis Books, 1982), 43ff.

9. Abraham, *The Logic of Evangelism*, 101ff.

10. For a helpful overview of these perspectives, see James A. Scherer and Stephen B. Bevans, eds., *New Directions in Mission and Evangelization 1: Basic Documents 1974–1991* (Maryknoll, NY: Orbis Books, 1992). For a sampling of contextual and liberation theologies, see William Jenkinson and Helene O'Sullivan, eds., *Trends in Mission: Toward the Third Millennium* (Maryknoll, NY: Orbis Books, 1991). See also Priscilla Pope-Levison, *Evangelization from a Liberation Perspective* (New York: Peter Lang, 1991).

11. See, for example, Alan Neely and James A. Scherer, "San Antonio and Manila 1989: '. . . like ships in the night?'" *Missiology* 18/2 (April 1990), 139–148.

12. Robert J. Schreiter, ed., *Faces of Jesus in Africa* (Maryknoll, NY: Orbis Books, 1991).

13. Ibid., 52.

14. Ibid., 54.

15. Mortimer Arias and Alan Johnson, *The Great Commission: Biblical Models for Evangelism* (Nashville: Abingdon Press, 1992), 78ff.

16. "The Original, Nature, Properties, and Use of the Law," and "The Law Established Through Faith, Discourse I & II," *Works* 2:39–70.

17. Outler's "Introductory Comment," *Works* 2:1.

18. *Works* 2:37–38.

19. For a discussion of this issue with regard to Wesley's Anglican heritage, see David Lowes Watson, "Aldersgate Street and the General Rules: The Form and the Power of Methodist Discipleship," in Randy L.

Maddox, ed., *Aldersgate Reconsidered* (Nashville: Kingswood Books, 1990), 33–47.

20. *Works* 2:28.
21. *Works* 2:28.
22. *Works* 2:30.
23. *Works* 2:31.
24. Emilio Castro, "The World Council of Churches' Ecumenical Affirmation: Mission and Evangelism," in *Trends in Mission*, ed. Jenkinson and O'Sullivan, 296.
25. Jimmy Carter, "The Task of Evangelism," *Journal of the Academy for Evangelism in Theological Education*, Vol. 3 (1987–1988), 7.
26. *Works* 9:70.
27. *Works* 9:70.
28. *Works* 2:39.
29. Bruce C. Birch, *Let Justice Roll Down: The Old Testament, Ethics, and Christian Life* (Louisville: Westminster/John Knox Press, 1991), 240ff.
30. Claus Westermann, *Basic Forms of Prophetic Speech* (Louisville: Westminster/John Knox Press, 1991), 11.
31. See H. Eddie Fox and George E. Morris, *Let the Redeemed of the Lord Say So!* (Nashville: Abingdon Press, 1991), 107ff., where some of these questions are directly confronted.
32. Schreiter, ed., *Faces of Jesus in Africa*, 57–58.
33. For example, Hans Jochen Margull, *Hope in Action: The Church's Task in the World* (Philadelphia: Muhlenberg Press, 1962); Alfred C. Krass, *Five Lanterns at Sundown: Evangelism in a Chastened Mood* (Grand Rapids: William B. Eerdmans, 1978); James Armstrong, *From the Underside: Evangelism from a Third World Vantage Point* (Maryknoll, NY: Orbis Books, 1981); and Mortimer Arias, *Announcing the Reign of God* (Philadelphia: Fortress Press, 1984).
34. For example, James R. Brockman, *The Word Remains: A Life of Oscar Romero* (Maryknoll, NY: Orbis Books, 1982); John W. de Gruchy, *The Church Struggle in South Africa*, 2nd edition (Grand Rapids: William B. Eerdmans, 1986); Cornel West, *Prophetic Fragments* (Grand Rapids: William B. Eerdmans, and Trenton, New Jersey: Africa World Press, Inc., 1988).
35. Jürgen Moltmann, *Theology of Hope* (New York: Harper & Row, 1967), 34.
36. Frederick Herzog, *God-Walk: Liberation Shaping Dogmatics* (Maryknoll, NY: Orbis Books, 1988).
37. See Elsa Tamez, "Wesley as Read by the Poor," in M. Douglas Meeks, ed., *The Future of the Methodist Theological Traditions* (Nashville: Abingdon Press, 1985), 67–84.
38. See Theodore W. Jennings, Jr., *Good News to the Poor: John Wesley's Theological Economics* (Nashville: Abingdon Press, 1990), 48ff. See also Manfred Marquardt, *John Wesley's Social Ethics: Praxis and Principles*, tr.

John E. Steely and W. Stephen Gunter (Nashville: Abingdon Press, 1992), 30ff. Cf. "Good News to the Poor," in *The Violence of Love: The Pastoral Wisdom of Archbishop Oscar Romero*, tr. & comp. James R. Brockman (San Francisco: Harper & Row, 1988), 219ff.

39. It is one of the important contributions of Theodore Jennings to have reopened this discussion in *Good News to the Poor* (see 140ff.). Cf. Marquardt, *John Wesley's Social Ethics*, 43ff., and Robert Moore, *Pitmen, Preachers, and Politics: The Effects of Methodism in a Durham Mining Community* (Cambridge: Cambridge University Press, 1974), 3–27.

40. See Guillermo Cook, *The Expectation of the Poor: Latin American Basic Ecclesial Communities in Protestant Perspective* (Maryknoll, NY: Orbis Books, 1985), 69–85.

41. Virginia Ramey Mollenkott, "New Age Evangelism," *International Review of Mission* 285 (January, 1983), 32–40.

42. *Works* 19:51ff. See also his sermon, "Free Grace," *Works* 3:542–563.

43. *Works* 2:38.

44. *Works* 1:169–171.

45. As in his sermon "The More Excellent Way," *Works* 3:262–277.

46. *Works* 2:494.

47. "The Large Minutes," *Works (J)* 8:310. Cf. Robert E. Coleman, *"Nothing To Do But Save Souls": John Wesley's Charge to His Preachers* (Grand Rapids: Francis Asbury Press, 1990).

48. See especially the sermons "On Eternity," "God's Love to Fallen Man," "The General Deliverance," "The End of Christ's Coming," "The General Spread of the Gospel," and "The New Creation," in *Works* volume 2, *passim*.

49. Theodore Runyon, "What is Methodism's Theological Contribution Today?" in Theodore Runyon, ed., *Wesleyan Theology Today: A Bicentennial Theological Consultation* (Nashville: Kingswood Books, 1985), 11.

50. *Works* 2:488.

51. *Works* 2:490.

52. Mercy Amba Oduyoye, "Teaching Authoritatively Amidst Christian Pluralism in Africa," in Meeks, ed., *What Should Methodists Teach?* 71–72.

Notes to Chapter 7

1. Xabier Gorostiaga, "Ya comenzó el Siglo XXI: el Norte contra el Sur," in *Educación teológica en situaciones de sobrevivencia* (San José: Seminario Bíblico/Programa de Educación Teológica-WCC, 1991), 80.

2. Ibid., 89–91.

3. Cf. Victorio Araya, "Samaritan Servanthood: An Option for Life," *North-South Dialogue*, 2/1 (Summer, 1987), 3.

4. Jung Mo Sung, *La idolatría del capital y la muerte de los pobres* (San José: DEI, 1991), 17–18.

5. Leonardo Boff and Virgilio P. Elizondo, "La voz de las víctimas, ¿quién las escuchará?" *Concilium*, No. 232 (1990), 369.

6. Pablo Richard, "1492: La violencia de Dios en el futuro del cristianismo," *Concilium*, No. 232 (1990), 429–430.

7. Hugo Assmann, in Jung Mo Sung, *La idolatría*, 14.

8. Cf. Araya, "Samaritan Servanthood," 3.

9. The phrase is from Eduardo Galeano in his book *Las venas abiertas de América Latina*, 2nd edition (México, D.F.: Siglo XXI, 1979), 3.

10. Pablo Richard, "La teología de la liberación en la nueva coyuntura," *Pasos*, No. 34 (1991), 3.

11. Cf. Victorio Araya, *God of the Poor* (Maryknoll, NY: Orbis Books, 1987), 91–95.

12. Cf. Jung Mo Sung, *La idolatría*, 96–100.

13. Cf. Franz J. Hinkelammert, *La deuda externa de América Latina* (San José: DEI, 1988).

14. Cf. Jung Mo Sung, *La idolatría*, 112–114.

15. Elsa Tamez, "Momentos de gracia en el Quinto Centenario," *Pasos*, No. 39 (1992), 23.

16. Because of the close relationship between economics and ecology, today we are beginning to speak of "the ecological debt" of the North toward the South.

17. From the well known Puebla Document (1979) final document, No. 1147. Cf. Leonardo Boff, "La nueva evangelización, irrupción de nueva vida," *Concilium*, No. 232 (1990), 510–512.

18. Cf. Araya, *God of the Poor*, 70–75.

19. Cf. Iganacio Ellacuría and Jon Sobrino, *Mysterium Liberationis: Fundamental Concepts of Liberation Theology* (Maryknoll, NY: Orbis Books, 1993), 216–18.

20. Cf. Araya, *God of the Poor*, 74.

21. Cf. Ellacuría and Sobrino, *Mysterium Liberationis*, 206–213.

22. Casiano Floristán and Juan José Tamayo-Acosta, *Conceptos fundamentales de pastoral* (Madrid: Cristiandad, 1983), 486–489.

23. "Declaración de Kingston," Nos. 1, 2, 3, 9, in *Cuadernos de Teología*, 11/2 (1991), 38–56.

Notes to Chapter 8

1. *Sermons CW* xxxii. Although it does not bear her name, Sarah Wesley is thought by most scholars to be the author of the Introduction as well as responsible for the publication of the volume itself.

2. Frank Whaling, ed., *John and Charles Wesley: Selected Writings and Hymns* (New York: Paulist Press, 1981), 29.

3. Erik Routley, *The Musical Wesleys* (London: Herbert Jenkins, 1968), 28.

4. *Sermons CW* vi–vii.

5. *Journal* CW 1:37.

6. *Sermons* CW xxiii–xxiv.

7. *Sermons* CW xxvii–xxviii.

8. Hetty was the nickname for Charles's sister Mehetabel.

9. *Journal* CW 1:108.

10. Stanzas 1–5 are from *Hymns for the use of Families on Various Occasions* (Bristol: Pine, 1767), #132, entitled "For a Family in Want;" see *The Poetical Works of John and Charles Wesley*, ed. George Osborn, 13 vols. (London: Wesleyan-Methodist Conference, 1868–1872), 7:157–8. Stanza 6 is from MS Luke, 56, and is based on Luke 4:26; see *Poetry* 2:90.

11. *Journal* CW 1:401–2.

12. *Hymns on Select Passages of the Holy Scriptures* (1762), 2:226, #364. MS Luke, 232–3, includes a variation of the first line: "Help us to make the poor our friends." See *Poetry* 2:157.

13. *Journal* CW 2:105.

14. *Hymns and Sacred Poems* (1749), 1:312.

15. *Journal* CW 2:84.

16. *Journal* CW 2:85.

17. *Hymns and Sacred Poems* (1742), iii.

18. *Hymns the Nativity of our Lord*, (London: Strahan, 1745; facsimile reprint with introduction and notes by Frank Baker, Madison, NJ: The Charles Wesley Society, 1991).

19. *Hymns and Sacred Poems* (1742), 83; see the 1780 *Collection of Hymns for the Use of the People Called Methodists*, #489, *Works* 7:676. Lines 4 and 5 of the stanza beginning, "Help us to help each other, Lord," originally read:

> Let each his friendly aid afford,
> And feel his brother's care.

The United Methodist Hymnal (1989) includes selected stanzas at #561, "Jesus, United by Thy Grace."

20. See Teresa Berger, *Theologie in Hymnen? Zum Verhältnis von Theologie und Doxologie am Beispiel der "Collection of Hymns for the use of the People called Methodists" (1780)* (Altenberge: Telos Verlag, 1989), 147ff., for Charles's emphasis on "feeling" and religion of the heart. An English edition of this work, translated by Timothy E. Kimbrough, is forthcoming in 1995 from Kingswood Books under the title *Theology in Hymns? Reflections on the "Collection of Hymns for the Use of the People Called Methodists" (1780)*.

21. *Hymns for those that seek, and those that have Redemption in the Blood of Jesus Christ* (1747), 8; henceforth cited as *Redemption Hymns*.

22. *Hymns on the Trinity* (1767), 15.

23. *Hymns and Sacred Poems* (1739), 118. See "And can it be that I should gain," #363 in *The United Methodist Hymnal* (1989).

24. *Hymns and Sacred Poems* (1749), 1:38.

25. *Hymns and Sacred Poems* (1739), 102.

25. *Hymns and Sacred Poems* (1739), 102.
26. *Redemption Hymns* (1747), 4.
27. MS Luke, 56; *Poetry* 2:90.
28. MS Matthew, 260; *Poetry* 2:37.
29. MS Matthew, 319; *Poetry* 2:46.
30. MS Acts, 421; *Poetry* 2:404.
31. See Manfred Marquardt's discussion of John Wesley's views on economic responsibility in *John Wesley's Social Ethics: Praxis and Principles*, tr. John E. Steely and W. Stephen Gunter (Nashville: Abingdon Press, 1992), 35–41.
32. MS Acts, 419; *Poetry* 2:403.
33. MS Acts, 74–5; *Poetry* 2:297–8. Stanza 2, line 1: an earlier version in the MS reads "abundant" for "redundant." For an edited version for contemporary hymnals see *A Song for the Poor*, 22–3.
34. *Redemption Hymns* (1747), 8.
35. MS Acts, 75; *Poetry* 2:298–9. It is interesting that Osborn omitted the first two stanzas above in his edition of the *Poetical Works*; he did include the third stanza with the fourth (not printed here), which appears in MS Acts.
36. See MS Preachers 1786, 1–4; *Poetry* 2:44.
37. See MS Preachers 1786, 19–22; *Poetry* 3:57.
38. MS Preachers 1786, 9–10; *Poetry* 3:49, stanzas 2, 5 and 6 of six stanzas.
39. MS Acts, 421; *Poetry* 2:403–4.
40. From the poem "On the Death of Mrs. Mary Naylor, March 21st, 1757," which was published in *Journal CW* 2:338, 339, 341; stanza 1 from Part II (stanza 3); stanzas 2–4 from Part III (stanzas 2–4); stanza 5 from Part I (stanza 2).
41. *Journal CW* 2:390; from the poem "On the Death of Mrs. Elizabeth Blackwell," Part I, stanza 3, and Part III, stanza 7.
42. *Journal CW* 2:407, stanza 7 of the poem.
43. *Journal CW* 2:407, stanza 3 of the poem "On the Death of Mr. Ebenezer Blackwell."
44. *Charles Wesley's Earliest Evangelical Sermons*, ed Thomas R. Albin and Oliver A. Beckerlegge (Ilford: Wesley Historical Society, 1987), 36.
45. *Hymns and Sacred Poems* (1739), 102.
46. MS Luke, 216; *Poetry* 2:152.
47. MS Luke, 220; *Poetry* 2:220.
48. *Short Hymns* (1762), 2:140.
49. Ibid.
50. Ibid., 2:226.
51. MS Luke, 144; *Poetry* 2:115.